30-Day Boot Camp

Eliminate
Fears and Phobias!

Kristen Baker

20660 Stevens Creek Blvd., Suite 210
Cupertino, CA 95014

30-Day Boot Camp: Eliminate Fears and Phobias

First Printing: September, 2008
Tradebook ISBN: 1-60005-114-6 (978-1-60005-114-2)
eBook ISBN: 1-60005-115-4 (978-1-60005-115-9)
Place of Publication: Silicon Valley, California, USA
Library of Congress Control Number: 2008934565

Testimonials

"I am so excited about this book! I have admired Kristen Baker's authentic and practical approach to working with fears and anxiety for some time. I believe that Kristen's approach to becoming interactive with one's own thought processes, followed by taking action in the moment is key to success in truly creating a fearless life."
Randin Brons, Ph.D., C.M.H., M.S.L.C.
www.ajourneytojoy.com

"Who hasn't had to face fears? If you don't want to be paralyzed by your phobias, if you want to go forward and reach your goals, you have come to the right place. Kristen brings you an amazing variety of studies and exercises that will help you overcome any fears you may have, and ultimately unleash the real YOU."
30dayBootCamp series created by Valerie Orsoni, CEO & Founder of MyPrivateCoach.com and LeBootCamp.com

"How do you ever repay anyone for giving you your life back?"
Shannon, Florida

"Countless therapist and other coaches did nothing, but Kristen changed my life and my world."
Carrie, United Kingdom

"My name is Robert and I <u>was</u> agoraphobic. I consider my-self a highly educated man that got blindsided by anxiety and fear. After contacting Kristen, I was skeptical as I had spent thousands of dollars on other programs. Kristen proved to me that I could conquer this and took me step-by-step through the process. After two short months, I was back to work as an engineer and living my life instead of fearing it. With her coaching, she transformed my life and helped me change my limiting thinking. Kristen can change lives and I am living proof. Always grateful!"
Robert, San Diego

"I began to do coaching with Kristen because her words were so real and I trusted her right away. After hearing her voice on the phone, I knew I had made the right decision. She is comforting, she is real, and she has been there. I had panic attacks for 3-years straight and once I started talking with Kristen, they got fewer and far between. I am pleased to say, after just a month of email coaching and 2 phone consults, I am panic attack free. Kristen brings so much to this disorder, she has lived it, she has recovered and now she is dedicated to helping others eliminate any suffering. The neat thing about Kristen is, she is casual, she is sincere and you really know she knows how you feel. I thank her for everything and I will continue to work with her with other issues."
Trisha, Wyoming

"I was referred to Kristen from a friend, little did I know that she was going to change my life. My life was chaotic and I had no self-esteem. My friend had told me she was using a coach and told me to email her. I did, and Kristen worked with me and showed genuine care. She gave me so many things to work on, and I realized many things about myself that I would not have without her. Today, I sit here and feel good about myself and I feel free from the negativity while my world is wide open. I am forever grateful to Kristen."
Susan, Minnesota

"I contacted Kristen with the hopes of her helping me to focus and learn to believe in myself. I was nervous at first, but after corresponding with her, I was at ease. I have done the email coaching with her and it has been so amazing! Seeing the words that she writes, sinks in. Her assignments are eye opening, but not confrontational. She makes you think, and learn, and apply. Kristen holds me accountable and gives me the strength to challenge myself, which I need. As a student, focus has always been a difficult task for me, but when I start to lose it, I can hear the words Kristen has said to me, and I regain my focus and motivation. My self-esteem has always been low because I didn't believe I could, but through working with Kristen, now I know I can. She has changed my thinking and has given me a positive outlook on life, I am forever grateful!"
Christina, United Kingdom

"Kristen is my angel. She made me feel so at ease and important. I was in a bad way and Kristen is the ONLY one that could show me the way back to living. She is the most caring and supportive person I have ever met. She is open and honest and she creates results. From not working at all out of fear, after working with her just one month, I had found a job and I am currently working full time. Kristen made me see my fears for what they really were and helped me to overcome them. How do you ever repay anyone for giving you your life back? You really can't except say Thank you and I thank you a million times over Kristen, you are my angel."
Shannon, Florida

"I have had the privilege of reading the 30-day Boot Camp while Kristen was still writing it. As someone that has had many fears, this book clearly identifies and breaks down the fears so you can conquer and move on. Had I had a book like this years ago, I would not have lost so much time in my life. This book WILL change lives and we should all be grateful for its creation."
Linda, California

A Message From Happy About®

Thank you for your purchase of this Happy About book. It is available online at **http://happyabout.info/30daybootcamp/fears-phobias.php** or at other online and physical bookstores.

Please contact us for quantity discounts at **sales@happyabout.info**

If you want to be informed by e-mail of upcoming Happy About® books, please e-mail **bookupdate@happyabout.info**

If you want to contribute to upcoming Happy About® books, please go to **http://happyabout.info/contribute/**

Happy About is interested in you if you are an author that would like to submit a non-fiction book proposal or a corporation that would like to have a book written for you. Please contact us by e-mail **editorial@happyabout.info** or phone **(1-408-257-3000)**.

Other Happy About® books available include:

Blitz the Ladder
http://happyabout.info/blitz.php
42 Rules of Cold Calling Executives
http://happyabout.info/42rules/coldcallingexecutives.php
Internet Your Way to a New Job
http://happyabout.info/InternetYourWaytoaNewJob.php
Tales From The Networking Community: Networking, Like Life, is a Process not an Event
http://happyabout.info/networking-community.php
"Foolosophy: Humor is The key to a Healthy Mind"
http://happyabout.info/foolosophy.php
42 Rules for Working Moms
http://happyabout.info/42rules/workingmoms.php
Wealthy U
http://happyabout.info/wealthyu.php
Happy About Being a Baby Boomer: Facing Our Newfound Longevity
http://happyabout.info/babyboomer.newfound-longevity.php
Rule #1: Stop Talking! A Guide to Listening
http://happyabout.info/listenerspress/stoptalking.php
Moving From Vision to Reality: Happy About Fulfilling Your True Purpose
http://happyabout.info/myfaith/vision2reality.php

Acknowledgments

I would like to thank my husband Tom for always supporting me in my endeavors and dreams. My son Austin, he gives me more inspiration than anyone I know; his perseverance and his never give up attitude are truly amazing from a 10 year old. My daughter Emily, her spirit keeps me young and alive and her humor can make anyone smile. In her I see such compassion and strength and she supplies me with such pride.

My mother, Barbara, who has never wavered on how far I can go in life. She has given me undying support and has told me to go for my dreams and believes I can achieve them.

Jack Canfield, his writings and teachings have taught me so much and have given me more confidence and excitement to reach my dreams. Although I have not met him in person, he has been an amazing inspiration to me.

Dr. Randin Brons, my true mentor. With his help, support and encouragement I have achieved my Master Life Coach Designation and my Spiritual Coaching Designation. He has taught me everything I need to know about coaching and I am forever grateful.

I would also like to thank and convey my appreciation to Valerie Orsoni, founder of My Private Coach, for being the inspiration that she is to me. She is a great role model for coaches and for every human being.

I would like to add a special thanks to Ava at My Private Coach. She has always been there to answer my questions with regard to everything involving this boot camp. She has directed me in this process and I am appreciative.

Although I have never met this woman, she has been one of the most inspirational women I have ever heard of. Her books are amazing, her spirit and her ability to let go of the past has influenced my life beyond words. Her name is Rhonda Britten.

The biggest group I would like to thank is my clients. They are the true inspirations. As a coach who specializes in anxiety, fear, phobias, and more, these remarkable people have beaten the odds from coaching and their desires to make positive changes in their lives. With each client, I am touched and forever grateful for your trust in me.

To

Austin and Emily

I love you with all my heart!

Mom

Phobia Free in 14 days
Free from P

Eliminate Fears and Phobias Starts Here!

free twelve gal fears +
phobias in 14 days

Preface

We all know that living with fears and phobias is a limiting way to live. In this 30-day boot camp, I will walk you through each day and teach you skills to be fearless. This boot camp is personal to me. As someone who experienced fears and phobias in the past, it is my mission to help others feel fearless.

Each day there will be exercises for you to do. These exercises will bring you clarity about your fears and how to overcome them. In today's world, there is so much fear, some are real, but most are beyond our control and therefore, should not be feared. It is my want and mission to help you leave the fear behind and move forward to a free and fearless life.

Fears and phobias are created by ourselves; they are continued and nurtured by us. There are numerous elements and reasons we believe about fears and phobias, but the single-most important element is, you can eliminate the fears and phobias for good.

This boot camp may not be easy at times, it may bring unpleasant sensations, and these reactions are needed to be free. On each page there is extra space for you to write notes to yourself and enable yourself to go back and read what you have written.

This is an interactive book and you may contact me via email at any time during the boot camp @ lifecoachkbaker@aol.com if you have questions or concerns. I am committed to your success and will walk you through all the way!

Allow yourself to be fearless and life will show you so much joy!

Introduction

What Is Fear

Fear.....It can be good and it can be crippling. Fear is an emotional response to something or a situation that caused you an intense fear reaction. The feelings of fear or the "fight or flight" is a natural reaction and is called upon when you are facing danger. This is a defense mechanism that is instilled in all of your brains, it is a good thing.

However, it is only a good thing when called upon in real danger. When you feel that fear reaction and sensation in everyday life, it is no more a good thing.

Do you or someone you know feel fear more than normal? If so, come along for the journey. You will not be fearful any longer!

DAY 1

Defining Your Fears and Phobias

Today is an exciting day. It is the day you start to get closer to a fear and phobia free life. This program is designed to be done daily, but if you would like to take more time, please feel free. People work at different paces and there is no right or wrong way to complete it, but it must be said that each day, you should be doing some part of the boot camp.

It is normal to feel apprehensive, resistance, excitement and also some mixed emotions, do not let that stop you. Today is a great day to start your 30-day boot camp to eliminate fears and phobias.

Take one day at a time, complete each section and if need be, repeat any lesson; please remember, for the most effective results, daily action is required. You should reserve 30–60 minutes on each day.

Here we go!

On the lines provided below, please list your fears and phobias.

_____

_____

_____

_____

_____

_____

_____

_____

_____

_____

_____

On the lines provided below, please explain how you feel when confronted with your fear and/or phobia.

_____

_____

_____

_____

_____

_____

_____

_____

_____

_____

On the lines provided below, please write a hierarchy of your fears, from most fearful to least fearful.

_____

_____

_____

_____

_____

_____

_____

_____

When we have fear, there are two types of fears, rational and irrational. There are many things in life that we cannot control; therefore, fearing them is literally a waste of time.

On the lines provided below, please write another list of your fears and phobias and next to it, write whether you feel they are rational or irrational.

_____

_____

_____

_____

_____

_____

_____

_____

_____

On the lines below, please write down your definition of fear and phobia. What it means to you.

_____

_____

_____

_____

_____

_____

_____

_____

Please take your time with Day 1, as it is the beginning to the end of your fears. Be as honest and clear as possible. Do not leave anything out, write everything down. This is significant to the elimination of fears and phobias.

2 Positive or Negative Thinking?

Now that you have identified your fears and phobias, we can start to break them down. Facing fears may not be comfortable and it can produce anxiety and very unpleasant sensations. These are only sensations, they will not hurt you.

On Day 2, we are going to identify whether your thinking is positive or negative. The way you think affects each and every fear or phobia you may have. To eliminate fears and phobias, we have to change the thinking as well as facing the fears.

On the lines provided below, please write down what you imagine when you think of your fears or phobias.

_____

_____

_____

_____

_____

_____

_____

_____

_____

_____

On the lines provided below, please write what your self-talk is when contemplating facing a fear or fearful situation.

_____

_____

_____

_____

_____

At this time, I would like you to go back to Day 1 and look at your fears and write down the worst thing that could happen to you if you confronted your fears.

_____

_____

_____

_____

_____

_____

As you go through the thoughts that surround your fears, I want you to understand that fear is a thought. Fear comes from a thought. You have created the fear by a thought, so that means that you can eliminate the fear by changing your thoughts as well.

Thought Patterns

3

D ay 3 is going to dig deep into your thoughts. Let me explain a bit about how thought patterns are formed. Negative thought patterns can stem from low self-esteem, negative inner critics (which often are our parents or a family member), association to the environment you are living in, and lack of attention.

When you do not have confidence in yourself, you do not believe that you can achieve things effectively. Doubting your abilities and your strengths create negative thoughts. Personal uncertainty develops, which in turn create self-doubt and lack of confidence.

For example, when you were a child, if your mom always told you were doing things wrong and concentrated on the negatives without validating the positives that you have, this will create overall low self-esteem and negativity.

As a child we all heard, "No!," "Don't do that, you will get hurt," "You did that wrong," "Don't be Stupid." As you grow older, those voices linger in your head and they shape your belief system.

When you think about something that you fear, you are visualizing a negative outcome, possibly from another exposure to the fear or phobia; this will keep the fear alive. Fears and phobias present in many different ways; it could be a fear of something that does not interfere with your daily activity, for example, spiders, snakes, or those that do interrupt your daily life, like driving or leaving your house.

No matter what the fear or phobia, they are all the same. They are created by negative thinking.

Below, please take a moment to write down your negative thoughts for the day.

_____

_____

_____

_____

_____

_____

_____

_____

There are always two ways of thinking, negative or positive. Take a moment and write down positive statements to replace the negative thoughts that you had today. It is important to make them believable to you.

_____

_____

_____

_____

_____

_____

_____

_____

When we were babies, we only had two fears, the fear of falling and the fear of loud noises. As we grew a bit, the common childhood fear of monsters in the closet or under the bed were created in our young minds.

As we grew older, the fear of the monsters, were no longer there, because after repeatedly checking in the closet or under the bed, we never found any monster; it was all imagined. The same holds true for many other fears as children or adults. All too often, there is the imagination of the worst-case scenario, which 99% of the time does not come true. Imagining outcomes of a situation is also created by a thought. Everything starts out with a thought.

Think back to when you were a young child and write down on the lines below, what your fears were.

_____

_____

_____

At what point did you no longer fear those things or situations?

_____

_____

What made you no longer fear them?

_____

_____

Are you starting to see how your fears have arisen? Can you understand that it is you who are creating your fears and phobias?

_____

_____

_____

One of the most vital things that I would like to have imbedded in your mind is: Just because you have a thought it does not mean it is true! Believing your negative thoughts will not move you forward. Your thoughts are coming from the pattern you have created.

4

What Are Phobias?

Welcome to Day 4.

You have now completed Days 1, 2, and 3. Great job! Always remember to go back and review the things that you have written and feel free to add to them as you move forward.

Day 4 is about phobias.

What is a phobia? According to Wikipedia:

"A phobia (from the Greek "Phobos" meaning *Fear*), is an irrational, intense, persistent fear of certain situations, objects, activities, or persons. The main symptom of this disorder is the excessive, unreasonable desire to avoid the feared subject."

There are different types of phobias; there are specific phobias, which is fear of a particular thing or situation. For example, spiders, snakes, needles, dogs, and many more.

Social Phobias: Fear of social situations, what will they think of me, will I make a fool of myself, will I panic?

Agoraphobia: Fear of enclosed places, fear of not being able to escape, fear of being far from home, fear of having a panic attack. Agoraphobia is the most severe of all phobias in my opinion. Being agoraphobic is truly avoiding the things in life that you fear and in turn, missing out on so very much even normal everyday activities.

It does not matter what your phobia is, because every phobia can be overcome. Some may take longer and may be harder to face emotionally.

As a coach, I have come into contact with many clients with phobias. In this one particular case, it is a woman, we will call her Sandy. She has an extreme phobia of vomiting (Emetophobia). She does not eat and has gotten down to a dangerously low weight because she is fearful that food will make her sick. Sandy has the irrational belief that if her stomach is empty, she cannot vomit. This is very untrue, it is actually better to have food in your stomach if you are going to vomit; therefore, it will not be as wrenching.

She avoids public places in fear of catching the vomit virus, she will not take medications in fear that she will vomit.

This fear has ruled her life and robbed her of normalcy and enjoyment. There is not a day that goes by that Sandy does not worry about vomiting. Every ache or pain she may have brings crippling fear.

Vomiting is not an everyday occurrence; it is out there in our environments, but it does not happen to an individual daily.

This is where the thought process really takes over and can limit one's life so dramatically that they are no longer living, they are just fearing.

Sandy has not vomited since she was 16 years old and she is now 28. Twelve years. She has limited her life, she cannot work due to the fear, she will not go places, she wants to homeschool her children and she is not living.

Sandy's fear has surfaced and remained due to her thinking pattern. This is how she has trained her mind to think.

I ask you at this point, do you have a phobia that is ruining your life? If so, please write it down on the lines provided.

_____

_____

_____

_____

Do you think Sandy's phobia is rational or irrational?

_____

If you were Sandy's friend, what would you say to her?

_____

_____

_____

_____

Now, look at what you wrote down as your phobia and write down what you would say to your best friend if they had this phobia.

_____

_____

_____

_____

_____

As I have had phobias that have limited my life for a period of time, I know how alarming it can be to face them; I know the sensations of the racing heart, the numbness in the limbs, the sweating, and the feeling of impending doom. If I did not face my fears and phobias, I would not be able to be writing this to try to help others, in essence, living my dream.

Facing the feared situation is the cure.

Building your confidence is crucial to allowing yourself to face the fear!

5 Why Are Some People Confident?

Each day of this boot camp will give you more insight on how to overcome your fears and phobias. As we begin Day 5, I want you to pat yourself on the back for a job well done thus far. Following the actions in this boot camp takes courage and strength and you are admirable for proceeding. I am proud of you!

Have you ever wondered why some people are confident and others are not? Have you ever resented someone for being able to just pick up and go and do whatever it is they want? When there is fear, these are normal emotions, but they are not healthy.

Ellen, who is a beautiful 24 year old woman, compares herself to her younger sister who is outgoing, bubbly, and has many friends. Ellen has found herself in a trap wherein she envies her sister and has hidden her fabulous qualities because she feels she will never be like her sister.

Ellen has a stutter and is very embarrassed by this; she does not socialize often, and is scared to look for a job in fear of rejection due to her stutter.

She wishes she did not have the stutter and she could be normal. Ellen is normal: she is intelligent, beautiful, kind, and caring, but she lacks confidence in herself.

During a session with Ellen, I asked her to face one fear every week. The first week, she did avoid, but the second week she was a huge success. Ellen decided that she was going to make some phone calls in the hope of finding employment. During this conversation, she was to stutter and not try to alleviate it. The conversation went great and she felt elated. She was not judged or prejudiced because she had a stutter; she was treated with respect and has had a new opportunity since that call.

Ellen could not believe that the phone call was as easy as it was; she had imagined that they would not talk to her, understand her, and reject her because of her stutter. The experience was nothing close to what she had thought it would be. This was an eye-opener for her because she proved to herself that it was her thinking and her imagined outcome that had made her avoid even trying.

In Ellen's case, her confidence was very low because she had the stutter and she was constantly comparing herself with her sister who did not have a stutter. She felt that she was less, but in my eyes, I think she is more. She has something that not everyone has, which makes her unique. Ellen would like to help others who have a stutter and I am certain she will do exceptionally well.

In our society, there are many cruelties. As children, we do not always understand why people are different, like in Ellen's case, she had a stutter. The inability to receive and react to the diversities that people have, often ends up in taunting or making fun of them. Naturally, growing up with a stutter or some other tic, so to speak, can mold your self-esteem and confidence into one that is quite unhealthy.

This is where many of Ellen's fears have originated from. She has feelings of being flawed and less than normal compared to others.

Comparing oneself to another is only a positive action when you are being motivated by that person.

Is there someone that you would like to be more like? If so, who and why would you like to be like them? Please list on the lines provided.

_____

_____

_____

_____

_____

What qualities and traits does this person or persons have that you would like to possess?

_____

_____

_____

_____

_____

As someone who was not always confident, I too envied people for having the freedom to do anything. I would look at these people and say, why can't I be like them? The answer is, you can be whoever you want to be.

It is quite like taking inventory of yourself and identifying what someone may portray that you do not. Somewhat of a de-cluttering of the negatives to get to the positives.

Why do you think some people have fear and others don't?

_____

_____

_____

_____

_____

_____

The answer to that is............

Confidence!

You can have it all if you want it and are willing to believe you can!

You can be fearless if you want to be!

6 Goal Setting

D ay 6, you are almost a week into this. Write down
what you have learned so far.

_____

_____

_____

_____

_____

_____

_____

On Day 5, we discussed a bit about confidence. We are
going to discuss setting goals. Setting goals and achieving
goals arc automatic confidence builders.

On the lines provided below, what does being confident mean to you?

_____

_____

_____

_____

_____

_____

_____

_____

_____

_____

_____

_____

The initial and simplest step to building your confidence is by setting goals. Write your goals down on paper and make them measurable in time, realistic, and attainable.

By writing your goals down, you can see what it is that you really want; therefore, you can devise an action plan to accomplish your goals.

By setting goals, I do not mean, writing down that you want to be a millionaire in 1 month. They must be attainable. Start out with the easiest goals to achieve. For example, it could be as simple as cleaning out your closet by the end of the week.

In the year 2000, I bought a new building to run my catering business out of and I had written down my big goal, that in 2 years I would have the house of my dreams. In 2002, we moved into a beautiful home, it is not my exact dream home, but it is much bigger with beautiful acreage; this in my mind is an achievement of my goal. Had I not written that down and made it visible to me, it may not have been achieved.

The act of writing things down is very powerful. Please write below what your goals are.

_____

_____

_____

_____

_____

_____

_____

_____

_____

_____

Are your goals measurable in time, are they attainable, and are they realistic? If they are not, please take the time and think about how you can change them to make them so.

If fear is getting in the way of you achieving your goals, this is a perfect time to set some goals in facing your fears. If you have many fears, take one at a time.

One day a few years ago, I had not been driving like I had once been and I had written a goal down that I was going Christmas shopping, by myself. As if it was yesterday, I can see myself driving down a very busy turnpike en route to the mall; I was shaky, but I was not giving up. I drove, I shopped and from that day onward my world began to open up once again. My wallet has gotten thinner too. In anticipation of achieving this goal, I had unpleasant sensations, I felt foggy, but I was determined to work through it. By committing myself to this goal, the thoughts and the sensations could not take my desire away. You too can commit to a goal and work through the unpleasantness that may come with the anticipation of achieving the goal.

This incident built my confidence tenfold. It was proof that I could do it and I had nothing to fear. This everyday act for most became the beginning of my confidence and freedom from fear.

Have you ever set out to do something and your anticipation stopped you? If so, please list and ask yourself, what really stopped you?

_____

_____

_____

_____

_____

_____

_____

_____

_____

_____

So now that we have discussed how important goal setting is for your confidence, grab your pen and write down your goals over and over again! Once you have written a goal down, no matter how big or small and once it has been achieved, your confidence will improve and you will be more motivated to tackle the next.

How You Dress

You may wonder, how your fears and phobias are related to your sense of dressing?

More than you can imagine. Everyone has a favorite outfit that they feel good wearing.

Do you have an outfit or a shirt that you feel good wearing? If so, write down what it is and why you feel good wearing it.

_____

_____

_____

_____

_____

_____

_____

As I think of this, I chuckle; this past Christmas eve, my husband and I were getting dressed to go to our family's dinner party. The closet door was wide open and the rows of clothes were hanging on the hangers. After about 15 minutes, we both had at least five outfits on the floor.

My husband was so funny because everything he put on, he said, "Nope, I don't like it." He did not feel good in anything that he put on. My outfit had been planned in my mind all day but when I put it on, I felt blah. So off went that outfit and back to the closet. More and more clothes came off the hanger until we both found the right ones.

We were late for the event because of our wardrobe changes, but what was important was that we felt good in what we both finally chose.

What you wear speaks volumes of who you are. When I see someone who is wearing bright colors, it makes me think they are happy and adventurous. Although I like black, it can symbolize someone trying to look thinner, that they are not entirely happy with their appearance.

When you dress yourself and feel good in what you are wearing, your mood will portray that. You will invoke and exude confidence.

For instance, most people going for an interview want to look good and impress their prospective employer. We tend to plan our outfit beforehand and we want it to be perfect and appropriate for the interview. We feel good about what we are wearing because it states that we are confident and professional.

If you do not feel right in what you are wearing to the interview, you will most likely not get hired. This is because you are not confident in your outfit and this will show in the verbalization of the interview.

Your clothes affect your mood. It is a fact. If you dress shabbily, this will radiate to others.

Everyone has certain colors that look great with their skin tones and hair colors, what colors brings out your great features?

_____

_____

_____

_____

_____

_____

_____

_____

_____

_____

When you look good, you feel good and in turn, you feel more confident. So when applying your clothing to facing fears and phobias choose something that makes you feel good, look good, and strong. This will help you believe in yourself more and enable you to take the risk of facing a fear.

When you shop for clothing, picture yourself wearing it, will it make you feel good? Will it look attractive on you? Will you be excited to wear it? Will you feel confident wearing it? It may sound funny to ask yourself these questions, but when trying to build confidence, it is very important.

How you dress is how you feel.

8

Loving Yourself

D ay 8 may be one of the hardest days. It is the evolution of learning to love *you*. You may think you love yourself or you may never even have thought about it.

What does loving yourself mean to you?

_____

_____

_____

_____

_____

Loving yourself is the "most" important quality you can have. To love yourself is to know who you are. To like what you see. To be grateful for what you have and are. To love yourself is not be conceited or arrogant; let us not confuse that, as being conceited, cocky, or arrogant is a shelter to one's fears.

To love yourself is to treat yourself with respect, to compliment yourself and to accept yourself for who and what you are. Being proud of yourself is an expression of love. Giving yourself a boost and telling yourself you have done well.

It is fascinating to me that as humans it is much easier to criticize ourselves and be fearful of complimenting ourselves. Criticizing and having negative self-talk will only keep you in a fearful life.

List statements that you tell yourself that may keep you in a fear cycle.

_____

_____

_____

_____

When facing your fears, if you do not love yourself, you will be very hard on yourself and will be discouraged if you do not succeed in the first try. This way of thinking will stall your efforts to try a second time.

Jonathon is a handsome and extremely intelligent man, who is learned and experienced in many things in life, such as traveling, learning different languages and cultures; in essence, he is a well-polished person.

Through the years, Jonathon has developed fears, fears that have led him to jobs that he is immensely overqualified for, fears that have not allowed him to socialize and forced him to live like a hermit.

Now, Jonathon has not always lived like this, he was a very social and outgoing man, but his thinking had changed and his love for himself was no longer there.

He has developed resentment toward others for having what he does not. He has this notion that people are better than him and they could never have gone through the hardships he has faced.

By resenting and unfavorable judgments toward other people he is not displaying love for himself, he is again reiterating his fears.

To love yourself is to fully accept your beliefs, morals, wholeness, and to accept yourself in your entirety.

An obstacle that can often be hard to overcome is believing you deserve to love yourself. If you were told you were not worthy of love or you didn't feel loved at any time in your life, this could be a hindrance for you.

I am here to tell you, that no matter what anyone has ever said or done to you, you are worthy of love from yourself and from others.

Please list what you love about yourself. For example, your eyes, your personality.

_____

_____

_____

_____

_____

Each day when you wake up, start your day by being grateful for sleeping in a bed, be grateful for having another day to live and succeed.

Each night before bed be grateful for the day you had. Be grateful for the food you ate. Whatever you think you should be grateful for, voice it to yourself.

When I was going through my period of anxiety and fear, I found myself looking into the mirror and telling myself

I was strong enough to conquer my fears. At first I would laugh at myself as I was not comfortable, but then I continued every day to go to the mirror and tell myself more positive things.

This became a habit for me to go to the mirror and tell myself what I liked about myself. To really look into my own eyes and see and feel the love I had for myself. By verbalizing it to myself while looking into the mirror, it really began to sink in.

The mirror exercise really brought me to love myself and it can for you too.

On this Day 8, introduce yourself to the mirror and yourself. Each time you go by a mirror, say something that you love about yourself. It could be your eyes, your cheekbones, your mouth, your hair, anything. Start to see the loving you.

Continue doing this every day, you will begin to love yourself and this is a big piece of the puzzle to eliminate fears and phobias.

Smile! Make faces! Laugh!

9

Your To Do List

Day 9 brings you one step closer to becoming free of fears and phobias.

A to do list is another powerful tool to build your confidence and alleviate fears and phobias.

You may ask why? By writing a daily to do list, you have in your mind what needs to be done for that day. If you follow this list, you will have a vast sense of accomplishment.

One critical element of your daily to do list is, to have positive statements on every other line. By writing them on your to do list and as you go through your day checking things off, you will see the statements and it will remind you of the positive.

Fear of failure is a very common fear; if you hold this fear, writing a daily to do list will bring you closer to success.

If you have fear of being alone and you have written a goal for yourself to be alone for a day, this is how your to do list will influence you greatly.

For example, you have decided that you are going to try to be alone; you write your to do list the night before when you are not alone and you are more rational.

Your to do list could look something like this......
1. I am safe alone and with others
2. Brush my teeth and rinse with mouthwash
3. I am more than okay
4. Get dressed in something I love
5. This is going to be such a great day for me
6. Do the mirror exercise
7. Smile
8. Mop the floor
9. Breathe and feel free
10. Put the dishes away
11. Think positive

This is just an example; you can put whatever makes you feel good on your daily to do list. It is important to cross off the things you have done on your list and to look at it frequently so you can see the positive statements over and over again.

These simple tools can have such a dramatic effect and do not involve a lot of work. You will feel empowered, you will be reminded often to not let your thoughts scare you and you will accomplish your list. There is no negative to this tool.

Getting into the habit of a daily to do list with positive statements will impact your life in a way you could never have imagined. You will feel more organized, you will start to have positive thoughts daily and you will build your confidence.

Write down a to do list for yourself with positive statements on every other line.

_____

_____

_____

_____

Similar to goal setting, you will be writing a list of things you want to achieve, but it is for each day.

Even now, I still write a to do list as I described and it really makes you stop and think about all the good things; when I read Smile, I really do smile.

This is a positive habit to develop and it is simple.

Every day write your to do list!

Finding Your Purpose

Finding your purpose is an opportunity for success, confidence, living fearlessly and having personal freedom.

Have you ever wondered what your purpose is in life? Have you ever asked yourself, "Why am I here?" I think we all have.

Please write down what you think your purpose is in life.

_____

_____

_____

_____

Why at this moment do you feel this is your purpose?

_____

_____

_____

_____

When we are growing up, we dream about what we want to be when we grow up, some go on to do what they dreamt about as a child, but most do not.

Wanting to have a specific career or do certain things does not necessarily mean that is your purpose.

How does one find one's purpose? There are many signs that show up in our lives that lead us to our purpose, but we may not even see them. Oftentimes we are not thinking about our purpose and what our role on earth is.

Everyone, everyone has a purpose. Being aware of the signs and patterns will bring you clarity toward your purpose.

When I was a young child, I wanted to be a psychologist, not a psychiatrist, a psychologist. I did not know the difference at the time; maybe I liked the word psychologist better. The only thing I knew was they helped people.

As I got older, I aspired to be a lawyer to help children. Frequently, I went through periods of wanting to be a nurse or a psychologist.

I never knew that my thoughts and dreams about these professions were signs of my purpose.

Although I did not go on to do either of those things, I am in a profession where I help people. I am a caterer. This means I cater to people; I help create and alleviate stress from their events and make them unforgettable.

As a caterer, I love what I do and the ironic thing is many of my customers tell me how much I have calmed them and taken the worry out of planning their event. This has been another sign of my purpose.

There have been clues along the way. Again, when I was going through my difficult time with anxiety, I was still able to help others. As crippled as I was with fear, the clues were still making their way in my life.

My grandmother had a heart attack and she had to be put into a nursing home for rehabilitation. While she was there she began to have panic attacks. She had every sensation that I had had and she was terrified.

As bad as I was, I drove myself to the nursing home and entered her room with 100% confidence and agility. She was lying on the bed with the look of terror in her eyes, I will never forget. It was my turn to help her.

Fragile and terrified, I rubbed her back and did breathing exercises with her to calm her down. She felt like crawling out of her skin, she needed to run, but I wouldn't let her, and she could not have done it anyway. Her adrenaline was so high and she needed to release it, so I had her punch a pillow repeatedly, and it made her feel better.

At the time, I never thought about my own anxiety, I only thought, I have to help her because I am living it and I know how she feels. After many other tactics I did with her, she was calm and relaxed and felt safe again.

As I left her room, I felt amazing, yet I was shaking uncontrollably. The very thought that I could help her while I was in need of help was so confusing to me at the time. Yet, it was another clue.

Please list the things that you enjoy doing.

_____

_____

_____

_____

_____

Are there things that come naturally to you? Please list.

_____

_____

_____

_____

_____

_____

_____

What captures your attention?

_____

_____

_____

_____

_____

What excites you?

_____

_____

_____

_____

What are you passionate about?

_____

_____

_____

_____

When you look back, can you recognize clues that may point you to your purpose?

_____

_____

_____

_____

_____

_____

When someone is living with fears, anxiety or depression, it is often said, why am I even here, I have no purpose in life. This is completely false. As much pain you may go through at times in your lives, as monotonous you may feel your life is, the fact remains is that you have a purpose.

Once your purpose is defined, your life will open up to opportunities; you will have clarity and begin to fulfill your purpose.

Finding your purpose will make you feel complete. You will have no fear as you will be guided by your Higher Self to your individual purpose.

When we have fears and phobias we are clouded and guided by the habit of limiting and damaging thoughts.

Facing a particular fear may have to be established in order to define your purpose. You have to be aware of the signs that are entering into your life and follow them.

Millions of people have the fear of flying, I was one of them. As a coach, I felt I had to face my last fear and my biggest fear before I could really coach someone.

We planned a family trip; originally, we were going to drive 12 hours to our destination, to avoid flying. That is when I realized I had no other choice but to face this fear to validate my purpose.

The days leading up to departure time, I had my share of irritable bowel and racing thoughts. Once I realized this had to be done for myself, my purpose, and my clients those symptoms started to dissipate.

Excitement had set in and I would only allow it to be excitement, I would not allow myself to think it was anxiety. Boarding the aircraft, I think I took the deepest breath ever. On went my headphones and out came my camera to take pictures from the sky. It was remarkable, after 15 years of avoiding traveling by plane, I was finally confronting the fear and winning!

After I came back from my trip, I knew flying was a sign for me. Deanna was given a free airplane ticket and accommodations to Hawaii with some relatives. She was scared to death to fly.

We had a couple of sessions and she went from wanting to cancel the trip to acquiring pure excitement and joy for this opportunity that had been given to her. Deanna took the long flight to Hawaii and she loved every minute of it.

If I hadn't taken the risk and faced the fear of flying, I would not have been able to help her in an honest way. This was my purpose.

Go over the questions from above throughout this boot camp and write down any more signs or patterns that come to you and define your purpose.

Hear and acknowledge the clues that your intuition is providing you.

Awareness will provide you information.

Do not dismiss the clues.

Taking Risks

Do you take risks or are you overly cautious? What defines risk to you?

_____

_____

_____

_____

_____

_____

_____

_____

_____

_____

_____

You must realize that everything in life is a risk. Even something as simple as ordering dinner at a restaurant, you may not like it when you get it or you could love it. Just to give you an example.

Without taking risks in your life, you cannot grow, you cannot achieve the things you want and you cannot fully experience life.

Without taking risks, you may never know if it could have worked. By taking risks, I do not mean to go run into on coming traffic, nothing that is obvious danger.

Not all risks are equal. Not all risks are successful, but many are. One will never know unless the step is taken.

A few years back, I wanted to buy a commercial building to run my catering business out of. This business was my mom's business before, but she had sold the function hall and I wanted to keep it going. I can remember asking my sister if she wanted to be partners with me. She is very cautious and is somewhat of a devil's advocate, she naturally declined.

After I showed her my business plan, she still felt it was too risky to put money up for it. I, On the other hand, I knew that everything comes with a risk, but I had the confidence that it would not fail.

Seven years later, I am still in business and keeping the name alive. I even have been voted Best Caterer in the state since I started.

The point is, had I listened to my sister, I would have lost out on my success. Furthermore, I never would have known and I would have always wondered.

This is what you don't want. In facing fears, even the simplest task can feel like the biggest risk, but in the grand scheme of things, you have nothing to lose.

Living in a fearful life, you already know the feelings of fear, so there is nothing new when facing the feared object, situation, or act. There is nothing to lose and only something to gain . . . . . Freedom from fears and phobias.

In the space provided below, can you list some risks that you did not take out of fear?

_____

_____

_____

_____

_____

_____

_____

In the space provided below, list what you may have achieved if you took a risk.

_____

_____

_____

_____

_____

_____

_____

Think about taking risks as expanding yourself. Think about taking risks as getting closer to personal freedom. Take a risk, as small or as big as you want. Start today!

Your Personal Belief System

This is one of the most important days of this boot camp. We are going to evaluate your personal belief system. You may ask, "What is a belief system?" In my words your belief system is what you believe to be true in your mind.

Your belief system is created by the quality of your thoughts over time. Most often, our belief system is molded from outside sources, that is, parents, friends, television, teachers, etc.

If fear and phobias are interfering with your life, most likely, your belief system is a major contributor. Let's see if we can identify your belief system and if need be, work on changing it to one of a positive and empowering nature.

As you developed your fears, what did your believe in your mind would happen if faced with the feared object or situation?

_____

_____

_____

_____

_____

_____

_____

_____

As someone who once had many fears, my belief system at the time was totally negative and pessimistic. Some of the common beliefs that I had had, were "I am not strong enough to get over this," "I can't do it," "If I do this, something horrible will happen."

These beliefs kept me in the feared state of mind. They were not empowering thoughts, they were fear-producing thoughts. It would become a cyclone of more fear believing these things.

When you are growing up, as a young child, the belief system starts to develop and grows throughout life, through experiences, accomplishments, lack of accomplishments and so forth.

Let's take the fear of elevators, for example. You have to go to the 13th floor of a building; surely you do not want to walk thirteen flights of stairs, but your belief system tells you that riding the elevator is a danger. You may feel that you will be stuck in the middle of floors and be trapped, you may feel claustrophobic, and you may feel like you will be trapped.

The fear of elevators commonly comes from movies on television, which is not real life or a fear of heights. It does not matter where the fear came from; your belief system surrounding the elevator use is the Key.

If you are scared of using the elevator what will you do if you need to get to the top floor of a building?

A. Take 13 flights of stairs
B. Avoid going to the building for what you need to?
C. Are you going to take the elevator and hold your breath until you reach your destination?
D. Other

If your belief system tells you that you will panic or get stuck in the elevator, this will not be a healthy and action-oriented belief system.

If you belief system tells you, you can do it, there is nothing to fear, you will ride that elevator with ease and possibly even enjoyment.

All of your fears and phobias, success, anxieties come down to your personal belief system.

Ask yourself at this time, why is it that most people can ride elevators on a daily basis and have no problems, closing the door and pressing the buttons, whereas, some people cannot even look at the elevator without becoming anxious, sweaty, and fearful?

The elevator is just one example, but it applies to any and every fear or phobia. Now, you may be wondering how I can change my belief system. There are several things one can do to create a positive, empowering, and healthy belief system.

1. Affirmations
2. Positive thinking
3. Changing your negative thought to the exact opposite
4. Taking responsibility for your own personal belief system
5. Eliminating any inner critic that may be hindering or sabotaging your belief system
6. Defining your own personal belief system
7. Believing in yourself
8. Believing in your strength
9. Believing in your wants and desires
10. Believing "you can"
11. Adopting an "I can attitude"
12. Allowing yourself to stretch and grow

As a coach, I work with many people who want to achieve different things. Let us take the example of Dan; he wants to find a girlfriend. His belief system is telling him that he will never find anyone to share his life with. His belief system is keeping him trapped in a limited existence because he does not believe he can meet a woman, he believes no woman will be interested, and therefore, he does not try.

Is this making Dan happy? Is this belief system productive for him? Will this belief system allow him to get himself out there and meet new people?

The answer is NO, to all of them. His belief system will keep him in seclusion, it will keep him alone and it will keep him in a state of fear.

Now, if Dan's belief system were to change, he would believe that there is someone out there for him. He would believe that he is of greatness and that he could make someone very happy. He would believe that he could go out and try to meet someone and have no fear.

Dan is living a negative belief system life, which is ultimately robbing him of true happiness. Dan states he wants to change his beliefs and thinking, but he makes more excuses not to and it is all brought on by fear.

You must allow yourself to believe in yourself, in your abilities, success, and actions and believe that what you think influences the actions that you take.

What beliefs about yourself would you like to change?

_____

_____

_____

_____

_____

_____

What do you think will work for you to change your personal belief system?

_____

_____

_____

_____

_____

_____

Are you willing to put in the effort to change your negative beliefs?

If not, why?

If you are, what steps should you take to do so?

Had I not changed my belief system when I was fearful, I would still be sitting on my couch in the fetal position begging god or anyone to help me out of it. The key is I had to do it myself. It was my personal belief system and I had the power to change it and so do you!

Give it a try! It will change your life.

If you do not believe you can conquer a fear or phobia, you will remain the same. If you start to believe that you can, the possibilities are endless. This is your choice.

A healthy and positive belief system is the catalyst to a fulfilled life.

13 Affirmations

You are almost halfway through this boot camp. Take a survey of yourself and how you feel about your fears and phobias now. Do they feel more conquerable? Do you feel the same? Do you feel more confident in your abilities to eliminate them?

Affirmations are what are keeping you in fear or helping you get out of fear.

Affirmations are anything we say to ourselves over and over again. We all have choices of what we affirm to ourselves. So on this day of the boot camp, I am going to go over the power of positive affirmations.

If you wake up in the morning and say to yourself, "I can't take another day of this," "I will never get over these fears," "I can't do this," you will undoubtedly feel defeated and attract more of the same limiting and disempowering thoughts.

If you wake up and start your day with something like this, "I am going to have a wonderful day," I am going to achieve and succeed," "I can do it," you will positively have more energy, drive, and success on that day. Guaranteed.

Positive affirmations work in transforming your negative belief system, and limiting ideas and can create what you want to get out of life.

You have proof that affirmations work because if you are residing in a world that is maintaining a life of fears, phobias, and anxieties; it is what you say to yourself that is keeping you there.

The repetition of the negative, limiting, fearful statements and thoughts that one creates will guarantee a life of full limitations. If you turn those negative affirmations into positives, you will in fact change your thought process, your belief system, and your "life."

Positive affirmations are to only be of positive nature. They must be in the present tense. They must be short and specific. An affirmation should always start with "I am" or "I can." Affirmations should never have the word "not" in them.

Affirmations are your own. You create them to fit you, your wants, and desires. Nobody can create the affirmations for you, but surely you can use some that others have created if they fit your life.

The critical component to affirmations is to use action words, one that will create emotion. Affirmations will change your thought process; it can take 30 days to transform and if you have the commitment and the strong will and desire to transform your negative limited thinking, you will.

As I had mentioned on Day 9 of the boot camp about a to do list, it is important to write down positive affirmations on every other line. Writing down your affirmations will give them power, it will enhance your mind as you read and reread them. Reciting and writing positive affirmations must be done daily to transform your thoughts and belief system.

Affirmations should be posted in all areas of your home, your car, your work, but most importantly, by your bed. You must repeat your affirmations at least three times a day, in the morning, the middle of the day, and before bed. When reading your affirmations, read them aloud and connect with them. When you cannot read them aloud, recite them to yourself.

Before you go to bed at night, read your affirmations repeatedly. The last 45 minutes before you go to sleep is the most important part of your day. This is when your subconscious mind becomes intoned with your thoughts and imbeds them into your higher mind. This is power.

Repetition is power. Repetition creates habit. Repetition is critical when using affirmations to transform your life.

When I began using positive affirmations in my life, it resembled a light going off in my brain that I had choices on how to talk to myself. Instantly, I felt more energy and hope to conquer my fears and become a limitless person. You must believe that affirmations can turn your life around as well. You must be active in this process and create the habit of utilizing affirmations on a daily basis.

At this time, what would be some positive affirmations that you could say to yourself? Write them down below.

_____

_____

_____

_____

_____

_____

As each day goes by, you may find that some affirmations work better for you; if so, stick to those. You may also add to your list any time. Affirmations are powerful.

Below find some examples of positive affirmations. Remember, they must be fitting to you!

1. I believe all things are possible
2. I can get over my fears and phobias
3. I am attracting joy in my life
4. I can do anything
5. I am successful
6. I am confident
7. I am fearless
8. I am excited to be alive
9. I have no fears
10. My life is filled with confidence
11. I am going to have a great day
12. I am strong
13. I have the power
14. I am changing my thoughts to positive
15. I am not limited in life

When you read these examples, how do you feel?

_____

_____

_____

_____

_____

Do you feel energy and motivation?

_____

_____

_____

This day of the boot camp is truly a transformational day for you. You can decide whether you want to change your thoughts and your negative affirmations that you have spoken to yourself to date or you can decide that the time is "now" to use positive affirmations.

This is a journey and you are the guide. Everything presented to you thus far in this boot camp are choices for you. If followed, you will create the life you have desired, as nobody wants to live a life in fear. Life is glorious and you owe it to yourself to share that glory.

Visualization

"Visualization is any technique for creating images, diagrams, or animations to communicate a message. Visualization through visual imagery has been an effective way to communicate both abstract and concrete ideas since the dawn of man." Wikipedia.

To visualize something is to imagine, to see a vision and results. Visualization is another powerful tool to use for eliminating fears and phobias as well as relaxation.

It is extremely important when visualizing a feared situation or phobia to stay in the moment even if you develop unpleasant sensations. By visualizing and experiencing the fear response, this will prove to yourself that you will be okay; although you may feel some unpleasantness, you would not have died from the act.

Describe in the space provided below what you visualize when you are creating for the feared or phobic situation.

_____

_____

_____

_____

_____

_____

_____

_____

Do you want to stop and run? Whatever you do, do not stop. Continue. If what you are seeing is unpleasant, you must change the visualization.

It is helpful at first to go through the unpleasant sensations to build that confidence that even though you may be anxious to face the fear, you are still safe.

When creating a new positive visualization for the fear, start out writing a list of what you want to see. How do you want your behavior to be? How do you want your reactions to be? Once you have brainstormed what you want to visualize, create it in your mind.

In the space provided below, describe how you feel after doing the positive visualization that you had created as your want.

_____

_____

_____

_____

_____

_____

_____

By doing this both ways, you will better understand that you have choices. You have choices in how to react, to perceive, and to accept the fear.

Back in my anxious, fearful state of mind, visualization was an action that I would do often, but it was not always the proper positive visualization. My visualization revolved, quite frequently around driving on the highway. At first I would see myself driving and all was well and then things changed, my legs would become numb, my heart would race, and the sweat and panic would set in.

My mistake at this time was that I would get up and go away from it so I would not have to feel the sensations anymore. This was showing more avoidance on my part, without even actively participating in the fearful act.

It was not until I made the decision to change how I reacted to the visualization that it changed for me. Going forward, I would use the same visualization but I would stay in the moment, I would actually calm myself down, proceed on the highway, and come off with a huge sense of accomplishment.

From that point on, I would do visualizations daily, but they were only of a pleasant experience surrounding facing the fear. I would see myself getting in to the car, turning on my favorite CD and getting excited about the new experience of driving on the highway. It would look like I was at ease and with complete confidence. I would enter the highway with no doubt or fear, it was empowering. I would do the same visualization repeatedly until my mind started thinking it automatically. As it did. When taking the real action and facing my fear of driving on the highway, I was able to achieve it with ease. The rewards were amazing. No longer did I feel trapped or limited. No longer did I feel different than others. I was free to go and travel where I needed to, as most people do.

Visualization to relax and de-stress yourself is pure power. Choose your favorite activity or vacation spot and picture yourself doing or being there.

Escape to the destination, where no other thoughts can come into mind. Be there in the moment and let those shoulders down and enjoy.

When visualizing something, make sure that you are using your five senses. What do you see? What do you feel? What do you smell? What do you taste? What do you hear?

My relaxation visualization has always been one of the beaches. My love for the ocean and beach is vast. It always starts out with me carrying my beach chair through the sand, finding the location for my chair that will supply me with what I anticipate. After setting the chair up, I grab the book I am reading out of my bag and I breathe in deeply to smell the salt water. It is refreshing to me. My feet are buried in the sand and I can feel the sand go between my toes, it is soothing. Hearing the waves crash is peaceful and amazing as well. I have yet to open my book; I am still taking in all the surroundings of my favorite place. As I watch the waves come in and out, I am in awe because I often think of the waves coming in and the tides taking away all problems, fears, and anxieties.

The ocean appears to be endless and it makes me think that there are endless possibilities. As I pick up my book, I am still in tune with the sounds, the aromas, and the feeling of the sand at my feet; it is luxurious.

As I write this to you now, I am at the ocean and breathing it all in. That is relaxation to me.

Create relaxation visualization on the lines below.

_____

_____

_____

_____

_____

_____

_____

_____

Use this visualization any time you may feel fear, anxiety, or you just need to relax and escape into your own dreamland.

This is your own imagination at work, revel in it, enjoy it, and be in that moment. Do not forget to make sure you are utilizing your senses.

You will see how amazing visualization is. Try it and make this your own.

15 Ask for What You Want

Asking for what you want seems simple. When it comes to fears and phobias, we often ask for what we "don't" want. By stating to yourself or anyone else, what you don't want, your subconscious will only pick up the "don't". Therefore, you will not receive what you want by saying what you don't want; for example, I do not want to be afraid of this anymore. I do not want to live with this fear anymore. If you don't want these things you must start the statement with: I want to be . . . . . fearless, I want to live an abundant life.

Just by the elimination of the word "don't" you will attract to yourself your want.

On the lines provided below, please list what you don't want.

_____

_____

_____

_____

_____

_____

Now, on the lines below, please list what you do want; if you have trouble, list the exact opposite of what you don't want.

_____

_____

_____

_____

_____

_____

_____

_____

Why stating what you do want is so important in achieving the things you want is because once expressed, you can attract what it is you want. If you are used to saying, "I don't want...." this is the very reason you have not gotten what you want.

In a feared situation, for example, let us t
vomiting. (Emetophobia) This is a very c
you are exposed to someone who has been vomiting,
you may say to yourself, "I don't want to vomit." You may
not vomit, but you will start to feel symptoms of nausea
and weakness, guaranteed. This is just one example.

If you do not want to fear things anymore, you must ask
for it. You must ask in the proper way to influence your
subconscious.

As my big fear was panicking while driving, before
I would embark on a drive, I would say, "I don't want to
panic," "I don't want to be scared." I did not know that
my expressions of the don't want would bring me exactly
that. It is a fact.

Picture in your mind the feelings and sensations that you
receive when you think of something you don't want. Do
you feel anxious? Does your heart start to race? Do you
start to sweat just thinking about it?

The solution to feel relief from these obnoxious sensations is to think of only what you *do want*. Are the feelings and the sensations more of excitement? Motivation?
Hope? This is how you should feel. The more you think,
ask, and speak of what you do want, you will begin a
cycle of only positives and receive what you want.

16 Taking Control

E verything in life is based on the choices we make. Most often, we develop fears and phobias because we feel we do not have control in the feared situation.

A perfect example of not feeling in control and often a common fear and phobia is flying on an airplane. We are the passengers and we have no control over the flying of the plane. That lack of control can make anyone go into a tailspin.

What many do not realize is that even though we are not the pilot of the plane, we are in control. We are in control of our thoughts, our trusts, and our beliefs.

You can take control of being a passenger of the aircraft by having your thoughts develop trust, confidence, and ease that the pilot is in control of the aircraft and wants to have a safe flight.

Your thoughts are so very important when wanting to be in control. Nobody can force their thoughts upon us. Yes, people can influence what we think, but only we ourselves have the control to make the thoughts come into our minds.

When you think about your fears or phobias, please identify below how you may not feel in control in a particular situation.

Please write down on the lines provided.

_____

_____

_____

_____

_____

_____

_____

Below, please write down what you could do or say to yourself to make you feel more in control of a feared situation.

Taking control of your fears, phobias, and ultimately your life is all about making the decision to do so. The decision must be made to change your thoughts surrounding the particular fear or phobia. There are always several ways of viewing things, you must view them in a positive light. This you have control of.

When I say "taking control," I reflect upon when I became a coach and I still had a fear to overcome. As a coach, I felt it somewhat fraudulent for me to coach people who have anxiety and fears when I still had a big fear. Taking control for me was changing my vacation plans from driving 10 hours in a car to our destination to flying. It had been 13 years since I had flown and each time I flew, I was anxious and felt not in control.

Yes, I had anticipation leading up to the departure day, but I was not going to let that stop me. It was final, I had my airline tickets, and I could not cancel. Two days before the flight, I took control of my thoughts and assumptions of this very big fear I was about to face. No more was I allowing my thoughts to go in a negative, scary direction.

In preparation for this big day, I had bought a bag of lemon head candies to suck on, I had my headphones to listen to music, and I had a book to read. My bases were covered as far as I was concerned.

The morning of departure, driving to the airplane, I had butterflies in my belly, but out of excitement and not out of fear. I had take control over my thoughts and sensations and this was only going to lead to me to success.

Boarding the plane, I will admit, I took a long deep breath and found my seat. The emotions and excitement I was experiencing were indescribable, I was facing a huge fear, and I was doing it for me and everyone else in the world. It was like no other feeling I had ever had.

The engines started and we took off, it was amazing. I had my eyes glued to the window and watching the disbelief in my children's eyes that they were flying was utter happiness.

Taking control, I did. The whole experience before, during and after my flight, I was in control. In control of my thoughts, whether they would wander to the scary, fearful side or remain in the positive, opportunity-producing side.

This was the best thing I ever did for myself, my family, my life as a whole, and for my prospective clients. This was truly a take control, fact-finding, fear-facing experience.

There is "no" longer a fear to fly within me. Why? I took control of the fear, it did not control me!

You have control over every fear you may have, you truly do. You are in charge of yourself!

So, on this day of the boot camp and forward, take back the control from the fear and no longer let the fear control you.

17 Don't Worry What Others Think

All too often we fear what others think or say about us. On this 17th day of this boot camp, my hope is that you will embrace your own identity and belief in yourself that you will not worry what others think of you.

It stems from loving yourself and taking control as well. Most people want others to like them and to think good thoughts of them, but so many times we are not ourselves and feel uncomfortable because we are trying to "fit in" and be accepted. This alone is quite stressful and essentially we are defrauding ourselves. If you are not yourself, then how can anyone really know the real you?

As long as you know that you are a good person and are moral and ethical, it should not matter what others think of you. If you tell someone about your fears and phobias and they judge you or make you feel bad, that person is not a worthy friend or acquaintance.

What are the things that you worry most about what people think of you? Please write down below.

_____

_____

_____

_____

Are you yourself with all people or do you tend to hide your true self?

_____

_____

Does it really matter to you what people think of you in the grand scheme of things? It should not. Typically, people who have any kind of anxiety, be it fears, phobias, generalized anxiety, or obsessive compulsive disorder are always concerned as to what others think of them. A common question to yourself may be, "What if they find out I have fears?" "Will they think I am crazy?" "What If I make a fool of myself?" It all goes back to that "What if" thinking; get rid of it, erase it, and you will stop second guessing yourself.

Deborah had a group of friends who were very successful professionally and she put on a charade when she was with them. She always felt like she had to be just like them, so she could never let them know she had many fears.

Deborah turned herself inside out for this and created such turmoil in her life that she became more and more fearful. She created the fear of people finding out that she was not as free as others. This tore her apart.

Then one day, one of the women that she hung out with, Amy, told her that she had a panic attack while in the grocery store. Deborah was shocked; she could not believe that she had an issue. From that day onward, Deborah let Amy know about her fears, some of which were stupid but existent nonetheless. She found out that this group of people that she had put on such a pedestal had their own fears and phobias. Deborah's world began to open up and she then felt accepted.

With regard to Deborah, she literally forced herself to be someone she was not in fear of being judged or ridiculed. As you can see, she did this to herself and she had no need to do it; they were no different from her, no better and no worse.

Trying to hide your true self is unhealthy, stressful, and in essence fraudulent for yourself and for everyone around you. Let go of the concern of what others think, what you think is what truly matters. If you are in a constant battle to please others and to fit in, your fears will grow at a greater pace.

Don't ever be ashamed of being less than perfect, because it is not possible to be perfect. Some fears are healthy and beneficial, but most are created by ourselves and are irrational; however, they are what makes you who you are and that is still of significance.

You can never imagine what takes place when you are open and honest with yourself with others. If you share your fears with others, 95% will confide they have fears too. It is healing and healthy. Even the most confident and powerful have fears.

Don't ever try to be someone that you are not. Keep in mind always that you are your own person and if others don't like it, you need not be associated with them. See your greatness and allow others to see it too.

DAY 18 Creating Positive Habits

reating positive habits may be easier than you think. On Day 18 of this boot camp, I want you to pay particular attention to the steps involved in creating positive habits.

Habits are formed by repetition; there are good habits and bad habits. There are habits formed by what has been instilled in your mind from childhood, there are habits formed from addictive products.

No matter what habits you may have, they can all be turned into positive habits. You may still have bad habits if you are not ready to release them, but you can also adopt several positive habits as well.

Getting up in the morning to take a shower and getting ready for work is a habit. Brushing your teeth when you awake is a habit. These are positive habits, but they are not the kind of habits that will eliminate your fears and phobias.

Please write below what your positive habits are?

_____

_____

_____

_____

_____

_____

_____

_____

_____

Please list below your negative habits.

_____

_____

_____

_____

_____

_____

_____

As you look at your negative habits, define what you can change to make them positive or release them.

The only way to create a habit is by repetition. Let us go over what habits you should adopt in everyday life that will help you eliminate fears and phobias and improve your life greatly.

1. Talking positive to yourself
2. Stop negative thinking in its tracks
3. Writing a daily to do list
4. Keeping a daily journal
5. Take "me" time for at least 15 minutes a day
6. Praise yourself
7. Wear the clothes you feel good in
8. Write down your daily successes
9. Eat five small meals a day
10. Tell yourself "I love you"
11. Be grateful for what you have daily

You should adopt just a few of these actions. Creating these positive habits will build your confidence and your security within yourself 100%.

One very bad habit that should be stopped immediately is surfing the Internet for answers on your fears and phobias. Do you look to the Internet for answers? If you do, do you ever get more frightened and possibly develop new fears from things you have read?

By looking to the Internet for answers and hoping for reassurance, you are keeping the fear alive. You are focusing on the fear, therefore, that is what you arc growing.

All too many of my clients search the Internet for answers regarding their anxiety. Every one of them has become more anxious after reading what others have or have gone through. The focus cannot be primarily on the fear. Looking for reassurance is actually hindering the process of eliminating the fear and phobia. You are your reassurance.

By creating, the habits that are listed above, you will gain reassurance from within. You will gain clarity, confidence, motivation, and freedom from fear. Please feel free to add more positive habits to the list.

It takes 28 days to create a new habit. These new things must be done daily for it to become a habit. You want it to become more of a way of life for you.

Do you think that doing these things will be hard for you?

_____

If so, what makes it hard for you?

_____

_____

_____

What can you do to fit these things into your life?

_____

_____

_____

_____

_____

You can start with the things that are easiest for you, then add others as you become accustomed to the easy ones.

These positive habits will change your life.

DAY

19 | You Are Your Own Safe Person

Let me explain to you that you are your own safe person. From my own experience, it was thought that if I had my husband with me, I was safe. This was a misconception.

Do you have a safe person?

If you answered yes, who is it and why do you feel they are your safe person?

_____

_____

_____

_____

When you are approaching a fearful situation do you rely on your safe person to make it better for you?

It is a comfort measure, for some reason we feel as though if our safe person is with us, we will be okay. Is this the way you feel?

_____

_____

_____

What is it that you feel your safe person can do that you cannot?

_____

_____

_____

_____

The real answer to that question is "nothing." If you are fearful of snakes and you encounter one, the same action will take place with or without your safe person. Your safe person cannot change anything.

It goes back to the reassurance again. You must look for reassurance within yourself; if it is there, let it surface.

You may feel a bit more anxious if your safe person is not with you during a time of want, but this is a good challenge for you. It is also a great way to show yourself that you can do it.

Let us take the case of Melissa. She was terrified to be alone. She had many irrational thoughts about being alone and she created such turmoil inside her that she was sure she could not stay alone. She feared that she would stop breathing if her husband were not at home. She feared that she would go into a panic and never come out of it.

This is a common fear among the anxious, but is it rational? No.

Melissa and I worked on building up her confidence in herself and her independence. It was perfect timing because her husband had a scheduled business trip and she had to face the fear of being alone.

She wanted to call a friend to stay with her, but that would not move her toward eliminating the fear. Having her friend stay with her was only keeping the fear alive.

Melissa and I worked on visualizing her being alone; she felt the fear and stayed in it. She then realized that she was okay after all. She was then able to visualize herself actually relaxing and doing things for herself in her alone time. Her positive visualization took her to a place of wanting to be alone. She felt more excited and confident.

The day arrived when her husband was leaving for his trip. She had mixed emotions on the day, apprehension, excitement and faith that she would be okay.

On her first day alone, she kept herself busy, she had kept her to do list with the positive statements on it and referred to it often. With each time, she became more and more aware that she was safe.

Her husband left at 8:00 a.m. on a Thursday and was not going to return until Saturday morning. At 3:00 p.m., Melissa looked at the clock and could not believe that she had been alone now for 7 hours and she was more than fine. Although, once she thought about being alone again, she became a bit anxious. This lasted for about 5 minutes she stated. She was now really beginning to believe that she was her safe person. Nothing different would happen to her if her husband were home.

Melissa's resources for help if needed were no different than is she was not alone. She began to enjoy this time. Her biggest hurdle was sleeping alone in the house. She had made a checklist of things to have near her had she needed it.

She had wanted to watch this movie for so long, but her husband said it was a chick flick and he was not interested. This was a perfect opportunity for her to watch and enjoy this movie. She settled in to her bed and put the movie in the DVD player. She laughed and cried during this movie and had no signs of fear. She was at peace.

That first day and night of her being alone changed her life forever. Although she missed her husband, she could have had a few more days alone. She now knew that she was safe with herself. She know longer needed her husband as a crutch.

This realization and growth that Melissa had made her relationship with her husband stronger, boosted her confidence and she was no longer afraid of being alone or going to places all by herself.

Melissa had great success. She will always be grateful for the time that she had to be alone; had she not been given the opportunity, she would still have the fear. The fear would still be alive because it is the unknown.

Grasping and really accepting that you are your own safe person is a critical piece to the elimination of the fear puzzle.

You are your safety! You and you alone!

20 Don't Put Off What You Can Do Today!

You have learned and hopefully started to ingest that you are your safe person and that your fears are self-made. We all have a million excuses not to do something at a particular time, we can justify it and we believe the reasons to be true and right at the time. This has got to stop when the action is facing your fears.

It is important that if you set a goal for yourself to stretch yourself and to face a fear or an uncomfortable situation, you must do it. Do not say, *tomorrow*, I will feel more up to it. Tomorrow I will be more ready. I don't feel good today, but tomorrow I will feel better able to go for it.

This cycle will continue and drag on to the next day and the day after and before you know it, you have lost more time and kept the fear or phobia alive. By putting off what you can do today causes more stress, anticipation and raises the fear level. Avoiding immediate action will only hinder you from conquering your fear.

This is a fact. It is a proven fact because I did it myself. This particular day sticks out in my mind. It was a Tuesday and I had written down that I was going to drive to the mall. I had done it a million times before without fear, but at this time the mere thought of it was terrifying.

It was in the early phase of facing my new fears. To do lists were written, goals were set and written and I was going to cheat fear. At least that was my goal for this day.

My anxiety was high the night before and I did not have much sleep. When I got up in the morning, I looked at my to do list and saw......#3, drive to the mall. "Okay, I can do it!" The shower went on, the anticipation started and I got dressed. Went down the stairs, looked at the sky and it looked like it was going to rain.

The anticipation intensified. The want was there in enormity. It was time. I grabbed my coat and my purse and off I went to the driveway. I got in the car, took a deep breath and turned the ignition. The lever went into reverse to back down the driveway. The lever went back to drive and I said, "Tomorrow will be a better day, I am off today and it is going to rain."

As I walked back into the house, my fear was gone and I was left with feelings of defeat and failure. The anticipation was gone, I was in relief mode, but all I was doing was putting off what I could have done today.

The sensations and anticipation would not be any different tomorrow, they will still be there and so what was the difference?

Nothing. It had to be done, whether it was raining, or I was tired, or I had a headache, it had to be done.

Tomorrow came and I was angry enough from yesterday that I gave myself no way out! I had no choice if I wanted to conquer this fear! I had no choice if I wanted to succeed. Today was the day!

The shower went on, I picked out bright clothes that made me feel good and I was saying affirmations over and over again. As I walk down the stairs today, I felt myself getting excited and empowered.

The anticipation was there, but I had chosen to dismiss the negatives. I was in control and I was not going to miss another opportunity to get closer to a fearless life.

The ignition turned again, the car was in reverse and I was out of the driveway. The radio was tuned to my favorite station and I was moving forward on the road. There were 10 miles to drive and I was going to do it even through the discomfort and fear.

It was drizzling and cloudy, but that would not stop me today. The odometer was reading 5 miles, I was halfway there. Deep breath in and exhale. It was happening, I was alone, I was driving, and I was safe! There was only one more mile to go. The butterflies in my belly were entering and I was excited.

The entrance to the mall was within eyesight. The sign said, "All welcome!" That meant me, too. Blinker on, right turn in and I was here. I had done it! In the rain, the clouds and through the fear, I made it to the mall.

On this day, my world opened up more than I can ever explain. Taking action today was the first day of eliminating this fear. It was proof to me that each time driving after this day was going to be easier and easier. Had I put it off another day, I would be where I was yesterday. Instead I was ahead, I was on my way!

The ride home was amazing! No fear, no anxiety, just exhilaration. This is no different than facing any other fear you may have. You can do it as I did that day. With each day, it gets easier and easier, but with no action, you will remain in fear.

Please write down below if you have ever put off what you could have done that day?

What excuse did you give yourself not to "do"?

_____

_____

_____

_____

_____

_____

What is the difference between today and tomorrow? What is going to be different with you?

_____

_____

_____

_____

_____

_____

When you look at your to do list and see an entry that says you are going to face a fear or phobia, do not put it off. If you are doing this boot camp, you have obviously put it off too long. It is proof to you and I that you want to be fearless. You must take action and not procrastinate. By putting off or holding off, you are losing precious time of living!

Don't be a prisoner in your mind. Don't do it anymore. It is normal and natural to feel the apprehension and the scary sensations when confronting a fear or phobia, but it is even worse to put it off because you are keeping the fear alive.

The goal is to get you living life instead of fearing it. Each day is precious and each day that is an excuse not to do something, is wasted time.

John, a client of mine, told me there were some things he wanted to work on with regard to his anxiety. It was refreshing to hear him actually saying the words, but the words that followed were ones of fear.

John stated that he would like to work on these things, but he was not ready yet. He would let me know them soon, but not now. The elation that I had when he told me he wanted to work on something specific was gone at that moment. He, again was putting off what he could do today. The sole reason....fear. What is he fearing? The sensations? Taking action? Or being fearless? This brings me to the next day of this boot camp.

Making the Decision to Be Fearless

D ay 21, wow you have come so far. I am so proud of you for moving forward. At this point, have you truly made the decision to be fearless? Living with fear is a choice as discussed earlier. It is a choice that is made by you. With each day that you choose to be fearful, it is not the fear's decision, it is yours and only yours.

With John, he was deciding he was not ready to release the fear he was hiding. He was only hurting himself by sheltering himself from it. John was trying to get himself ready to divulge his fear, and he was holding back. This was because, once he did, he was aware that he would have to face it.

As in the day I drove to the mall, I made the decision to feel the fear and move toward fearlessness. Is anyone ever ready to face a fearful situation? If you think about the fear in a negative way you will never make the decision to go forward.

Think for a moment about all the men and women fighting for our country in Iraq. Do you think they were ready to go on the battlefield? Do you think they were fearless? Thousands of lives have been lost in this war. It is a huge risk, but each individual fighting over there has made the decision to sign up in the military and have a goal at the end.

These amazingly brave people have stood by their decision despite fear, anxiety, anguish, and despair. They all made a decision and it is final. They will live with the decision and be proud of it.

Sure not all military signed up thinking that fight was imminent, but they knew it was always possible. The lesson here is that these incredible people made the decision and did not back out in the face of fear!

The same goes for everyone who has a fear or phobia. The decision is yours to stay in fear or to embrace it and move through it. Remember John, he is wasting precious time by not coming forward with his fear that he wants to work on, in the near future.

On the lines below, please write down if you have made the decision to be fearless?

If you have not, what is holding you back?

_____

_____

_____

_____

_____

Look back at your answer and identify if this is an excuse because of fear?

_____

_____

Through the last 20 days, we have gone over things that will help you face your fears and phobias; what tools can you apply at this point to help you make the decision to be fearless?

_____

_____

_____

_____

Which tool makes you feel most empowered?

_____

_____

Think about when you were a baby. Many decisions had to be made and there were a lot of unknowns and first times.

When you were a baby, you started to crawl. That first crawl had to have been a series of mixed feelings. Excitement along with fear and confusion. As a baby, you continued to move forward and crawl all over. The crawl was the first step to the walk.

Even as babies, we had crutches and our safety person. You go from crawling to mom or dad to a walking aid, commonly a push toy. This is helping you get ready for the first step on your own.

Think about if you were this baby right now, what would be going through your mind thinking about taking that first step?

_____

_____

_____

_____

_____

You, as a baby have got to make a decision whether you are going to take that first step. Your mom can coach you all the way and try to coerce you into taking the step, but ultimately it is your decision. Once you make the decision to take that first, independent step, there is no going back. The decision was made and you have to bring the next foot forward. Once the second foot is even with the first, you have taken your first step. The second step becomes much easier. Before you know it, you are running.

This process applies to all babies, toddlers, teens, and adults. Each first experience supplies us with sensations; it is how you perceive these sensations that will determine your next step.

Have you ever experienced a baby taking its first step?

Were you in front of him or her telling them they could do it?

Did you say, c'mon, there is nothing to be afraid of, put one foot in front of the other?

The same as you have done with a baby, you can do to yourself. Always know if you put one foot in front of the other, you will be one step closer to a fearless and phobic free life.

You can do it just like that baby took his/her first crawl and moved on to the first step! There is no difference; it is all your decision to take it!

Desensitizing

In previous days of this boot camp, you have been asked to identify your fears and phobias, determine when you acquired them, why you feel you have them. We are going to discuss desensitization on Day 22.

Desensitization is the opposite of addiction and although not often compared, fear is an addiction of sorts. Our minds and our environments keep the fear alive, which is equal to addiction. Desensitization is the process in which one takes action toward the release of the addiction or the fear reaction.

It is very similar to becoming sensitive to certain household products or other irritants. If you were cleaning with bleach, for example, and you broke out in a rash and had labored breathing, you would avoid using that product again, am I correct?

By having a negative reaction to this chemical, you have become sensitized to it, so it would be natural to discontinue use to eliminate the unpleasantness that it caused you.

In comparing the example from above to fears and phobias, the same process is followed. When there are fears or phobias you have become sensitive to the situation, object, or act. Something triggered a negative, fearful response in you which created the fear. Let's look at the events of September 11, 2001. Everyone experienced some sensitizing to this dreaded day.

This day changed the lives of so many and developed a magnitude of fears. We were all told to be vigilant, to more or less look over our shoulders. We were also told to be cautious when flying or being in crowds. We were told that we were a vulnerable country. Albeit the horrific acts of September 11, 2001, were just that, horrific, the media sensitized us to these fears.

Looking back, I remember avoiding this Holiday Stroll because there was a crowd of thousands of people and one never knows who may be lurking in there. The immediate response to this situation was to stay close to home, avoid crowds, and avoid airports or travel of any kind for that matter.

Were the fears justified during this time? Millions think they were. This event was one that we were unfamiliar with, so the reaction and the emotions surrounding it were unclear. So fear developed and with good reason. However, keeping the fears alive would only make the terrorists more powerful and hence, cripple us as individuals and a society if we continued living in fear.

In honesty, I had to make a decision when the Holiday Stroll came to pass again whether I was going to face it and attend. In my thinking of going to this glorious event, my heart would pound and the thoughts would pour into my head, none of which were supportive of my attendance to this event.

Then I asked myself a question. That question was, "Am I going to let something I have no control over rob me and my family of creating memories and enjoyable times?" At that moment, my decision was made; I was going to the Holiday Stroll. When the day came, I did try to make excuses that it was too cold and I was tired. These excuses were not only going to deprive me and my family of having a wonderful time, but they were programming my mind that this is something to fear. Not only this event, but any other event where large crowds are present. I could not allow that.

As we pulled up to park I saw the streets crowded with people, my heart began to race, I became dizzy and unsure. As I took one step closer to joining the crowd, I took many deep breaths and told myself I could do it. The anxiety and the sensations subsided by the time I had reached the crowd.

It cannot be said that I did not look around at everyone and wondered if something was going to happen that evening but the key was, I was there, I was participating, my children were having a barrel of fun and I was there.

The night went on for hours with different venues all of which had huge crowds of strangers. Each minute I was there I was desensitizing myself to the large crowds. By the end of the evening, those invasive, scary thoughts were no longer present within me.

The key element of my desensitization was to feel the fearful sensations and have the fearful thoughts and continue on anyway. Allowing myself to relax and breathe to calm myself was crucial to moving on.

Let's take driving fears in this instance. Driving fears are among one of the greatest fears and the most widely avoided acts. So many elements can contribute to the formation of this fear. You may have been involved a car accident; you may have gotten lost and had a panic attack; whatever the case may be the fear has been created.

Once you have had the fear response while driving, it can be crippling and it can be tough to erase that feeling and association, so the easiest and the best thing we *think* we should do, is not to do it anymore; therefore, we will not experience the intense fear. It may sound logical, but it is not rational.

Whatever occurred in millions of people to create the fear of driving was a sensitization. How does one become desensitized? The only way to desensitize yourself is by exposure. It does not matter what the fear or phobia is, exposure is the cure. Exposure does not inevitably mean to jump right into the situation in full force. It can be done in steps.

It is imperative when exposing yourself to a fear or phobia that you are eager to accept that it may not be comfortable at first. You will feel uneasy. You may want to turn around and run from it. You need to prepare yourself for the exposure and believe you can get through it.

It is of utmost significance to be relaxed while starting the exposure. You must be able to calm yourself through the process. It has to come from you. You are the captain of the ship and you are in control. Do not expect too much from yourself; set a goal of how far you want to go and do it gradually if need be.

One step at a time, as we discussed earlier. By taking the small steps you will start the desensitizing process. It is not necessary to tackle a fear head on, but it is true that doing nothing will keep it alive.

Write down below, what the fear or phobia is and create a list of what steps you want to take to expose yourself.

_____

_____

_____

_____

_____

_____

_____

_____

It doesn't matter what the fear may be, you can begin by looking at pictures, you can than envision yourself in the feared situation, you can enter into the fear on a limited basis at first. By doing these things you will be on your way to becoming desensitized.

Going to the dentist is another fear that many people have. It is not known why, but it is a very common fear. You may ask how you should desensitize yourself from the dentist, if you are afraid to go?

Start out slow. Make an appointment to go into the office, with no scheduled procedures. Have the staff show you around, sit in the dental chair and relax. Feel the fear and use the techniques you have to calm yourself.

The next step would be to go to the dentist with a family member or a friend and watch. This will show you that they are okay. Once you feel at ease, make an appointment for yourself for a simple cleaning. You will see how amazing your teeth feel and you will prove to yourself that you were okay.

Repetitive exposure is the key to overcoming the fears and phobias. Taking steps will desensitize you and you will no longer have the fear.

Write down at this point, have you ever reentered a situation that you had a bad incident with in the past?

_____

What made you follow through the reentry process?

_____

_____

_____

_____

_____

_____

You can pursue those same steps as you performed before in facing the fear or phobia.

The addressing of this topic again is to have you more prepared as we complete this boot camp.

Recap:

1. Write down a list of goals or steps that you want to take to expose yourself
2. Reward yourself and your mind for the success that you had on each step
3. Visualize a positive outcome
4. Feel the fear and take a step forward, using relaxation techniques
5. Continue exposing yourself more and more each time
6. Recognize the results when you have fully exposed yourself

It is vital to keep your eye on the end result. Each time you expose yourself to fear or phobia it will get easier and less fearful. Frequent exposure is the key to eliminating fears and phobias.

You can do it! Action is what is needed! You have to start someplace and reward yourself all the way.

You are by no means alone as you have this boot camp to help you through! You are the master of your life.

Keeping Track of Your Personal Successes

Every day in each of our lives there is success. Success happens in numerous ways. For most of us, we do not even consider that each task accomplished is a success.

As I talked previously about *to do lists*, each item on the list that has been completed is a success. What I would like you to do at this point is write down your daily success from hereon.

It does not matter if you don't think it is a success, if it is something you wanted to achieve, whether it be going to the bank or cleaning your bedroom, write it down as a success.

Keep a daily success chart along with your to do list; you can have it in the same book. It is recommended to have a notebook of your daily to do list, and on each back side write your daily successes.

The power this will give you is immeasurable. You may not notice it instantly, but as you continue with this and create the habit, you will without doubt feel a boost in your confidence.

If you are someone who has trouble following through or procrastinating, keeping track of your successes will increase your capacity to end that and look forward to more success. When you start to see your daily successes it will prove to you that you can achieve and you carry out anything.

When I say anything, I mean even the hardest tasks for you, which I assume is facing your fears or phobias. When preparing your to do list, remember to always put something on the list that will allow you to stretch yourself, even if it is minute.

As you start to see your daily successes having more impact, you will know that you have stretched yourself more than before. Let us take the example of Jim:

He stays up all night long as he works from late afternoon well into the night. He wants so much to find a new job, but he sleeps until noon every day. This sleep schedule has impacted his job search. He has tried alarm clocks, with no success. Jim is discouraged with himself and his pattern of going to sleep so late and not being able to get up at a sensible time in the morning.

We worked on him really wanting to wake up earlier so he could be pro-active in the job search; he knew this had to happen. He wrote it to me numerous times and his frustration was evident.

Jim finally had an interview. It was a concern of mine that he would not wake up in time but he mentally prepared himself to do so and he did it with no problem. He had something to wake up for. Since the interview, he has been able to wake up each morning without an alarm clock around 9:00 a.m. This is success. It may seem silly to some, but not to Jim or myself; I think it is a massive success for him.

Write down below what your successes are today.

_____

_____

_____

_____

_____

_____

_____

When keeping the success log, make sure to take at least 20 minutes every two days to review your successes. Smile and realize every day you have personal successes, some big, some small, but all successes.

When your successes involve eliminating your fears or phobias, make that stand out. Color them in bright colors or put stickers to highlight a huge success. Visit this page often to remind yourself of your strengths and dedication.

Also keep in mind that failures contribute to personal success. If you have set out to do a task and you have not accomplished it, don't beat yourself up. You will most likely have greater motivation to do so the next time. Keeping track of your personal successes will undeniably swell your confidence level. When you have confidence, you can achieve everything, this includes becoming fearless.

It is easy to track your personal daily successes. Make this a habit. It cannot be expressed how this will, by and large, increase your positive mindset and motivation. Every day is a success. Every action is a success because it was taken. As simple as keeping a personal success log may seem, it is a success.

Write down below what you want your personal successes to be.

_____

_____

_____

_____

_____

_____

If you achieved these successes, how would you feel?

_____

_____

_____

_____

Why would you feel like this?

You have got to believe in your personal success. Each success brings greater and greater successes.

In this log you are now going to maintain, write down and acknowledge whatever *you* feel is a success. Your personal successes will not be the same as someone else's, that is why it is your personal success log.

When facing a fear or phobia you must remember even thinking of combating the fear is a success. You are a success!

You are a success!

DAY 24 Accepting Imperfection

Millions of people develop fears by trying to be perfect. The newsflash is there is no such thing as perfect. There is no perfect person, no perfect way to do something, there is just no perfect.

The key on Day 24 of this boot camp is to release the need and want to be perfect and accept imperfection. Accepting imperfection is not to be slack or not put in any effort; it is to accept that you can only do the best you can do. Your best is perfect, your own perfect.

Perfectionism has become somewhat of an epidemic. We are all trying to do everything and have things perfect. The amount of stress and anxiety this causes is enormous. Nothing is ever completely perfect; it just needs to be acceptable to you.

It is funny, when I had my anxiety, I did not want anyone to know. Never did I want people to know that I was deeply flawed at the time. Trying to keep the charade of a confident, fearless person created more fear and anxiety for me.

For a period of time, I was ashamed of my imperfections; it was a difficult period of my life. This had to change. I changed myself by exposing my imperfections and I came clean, so to speak, about my anxiety and my limitations at the time.

As I started this process, I felt like the monkey was off my back; the cat was out of the bag and I was on my way to freedom. It created such opportunities for me to be myself. The greatest part of it all was that I was still accepted and respected with my imperfections.

Please write down below what your definition of perfect is.

_____

_____

_____

_____

_____

In your mind, is perfect within reach?

_____

_____

Is being perfect important to you and if so, why?

This brings me to Nancy. She has a great career, her children attend private schools and she drives a fancy car. On the outside it seems like Nancy has the perfect life. This is not the case at all. She is buried in debt, she is unhappy but she is willing to accrue more debt to keep appearances up. In this case, Nancy will probably, in the end, lose her home, her fancy car, and have her children attend public school. What do you think will happen to Nancy? Will others find out she is not perfect?

Nancy is hurting herself and her family by not accepting imperfections. Eventually, it will crash down on her and the effects will be massive. Do you see my point?

Accepting your imperfections is going to lift the weight off your shoulders. This also relates to fears and phobias and by accepting you have them, you are not perfect, no one is.

Once I exposed myself as having anxiety and fears, I found that I was not alone at all. The most confident people I knew had it too. It is all around you and you probably don't even know it because as humans, we are so afraid to reveal our flaws.

Having fears and phobias is not a flaw; in actuality any one who has them is an extremely strong person. You have to be courageous to live with these horrific sensations and fear responses and continue on toward a fearless life. It is not easy to live with fears.

Let it be known that perfection is the standards you set for yourself. Your own is the key, not what others think it should be, yours and yours alone.

As a caterer, I often hear when I cater to a wedding that it was a perfect meal. It was not perfect by definition, I am certain something could have been done better, but it was perfect in their mind because that is how they envisioned it to be.

Have you ever said something was perfect? If so, what was it and what made it perfect to you?

_____

_____

_____

_____

_____

_____

Do you understand how important it is to accept imperfections?

Relieving your personal stress and accepting that each one has his own standards of perfection will bring you closer to freedom. As I write this boot camp, do I think it will be perfect? No. Would I like it to be perfect, yes, but it will not happen. Each reader will view it differently; therefore, there is no way to achieve perfection and that is okay with me. It is important for my readers to come out of this boot camp with at least one thing positive and that is perfect to me. If my writing can help each reader in some way, that is my perfect. I accept that not all readers will agree with all that I have said, as much as I would want them to; I am realistic enough to know otherwise.

In all honesty, who wants to really be perfect anyway; it is such a constant and laborious process.

Accept your own personal imperfections, be proud of them, and allow yourself to be less than perfect.

DAY 25

Expressing Your Feelings

Day 25, congratulate yourself for coming this far. How are you feeling about this process so far?

_____

_____

Day 25 is about expressing your feelings. When a person has fears, phobias, or anxiety disorders it usually stems from feelings. A feeling one has affects the whole body. Most often the feelings are not confronted or exposed. This is when it becomes a predicament.

Feelings can present as happiness, sadness, excitement, anger, and embarrassment to name just a few. Have you ever heard this expression, "I am so excited I could burst?" This statement alone is telling you, you need to let your feelings out or you will burst. The same goes for anger, "I am so angry I could scream." Again, showing you, above all, keeping feelings in is affecting your whole body.

What happens when we suppress our feelings? They build and build until we cannot take it anymore; this in itself can create anxiety, fear, low self-esteem, and depression.

If you have feelings of happiness, shout it out, share it with the world, you have the right. If you feel anger, you must release it by confronting the subject that made you angry or write it down or punch a pillow. The importance is to release your feelings and let them out.

Let's say that you have an argument with a friend and you hold those feelings inside, they will fester and brew and cause you more anger and uneasiness toward the person. The best way to rid yourself of the anger is to discuss it with the friend but even if you don't, writing it down will release it as well. Suppressing your feelings, be they good or bad, is not a healthy act.

Last year, I worked with this woman, Sherry, who was so excited about getting this new job. It was in marketing and she was ecstatic that she got this position from this particular company. She held her feelings in from her parents because she knew that her parents wanted her to go into another field.

This was unfortunate for Sherry because she felt that she could not share her delight over this new job with them. It was also unfortunate for the parents because they had chosen to disapprove of her career choice, in essence missing out on this wonderful time for her.

Sherry's excitement quickly turned to anger, sadness, and fear that her parents were going to be very angry with her. In an instant, her feelings had changed. What we worked on was her keeping a journal and expressing all her feelings in it surrounding this one event. The first day she wrote for hours, she had never written in a journal before but she found herself releasing much more than she set out to.

After just 24 hours, Sherry felt lighter. She identified her feelings and why she was having them and began to accept them. As it turned out, her last entry in the journal on that first day reverted back to her excitement! This was mind boggling to her due to the anger and sadness that she had when she put pen to paper.

Expressing your feelings is powerful.

Sadness is another feeling that is commonly suppressed. You may not want anyone to see you cry or wonder what is wrong, so you bury the sadness deep inside you.

This will undoubtedly hurt you in the end, both physically and mentally. Feelings of sadness are normal and deserve reaction to. If you need to dry to let it out, do so. Write it down if you want to. Do whatever you feel will help you express the feeling.

It is often said that feelings of excitement create butterflies in your belly, a racing heart, and sweating much the same way as panic does. In fact, the feelings that your body has are identical to a panic attack.

Can you think of a time that you held your feelings in because you were embarrassed of them? Please explain below.

_____

_____

_____

_____

_____

_____

Can you write down if you have a tendency to hold your feelings in, if so why?

_____

_____

_____

_____

Have you ever wanted to say something and you held back and then wished you had said how you felt?

At this point, I would like you to ask yourself what you are feeling this moment and write it down.

_____

_____

_____

Along with expressing your feelings, I want you to always remember, you cannot have a feeling without a thought first. Your feelings arrive solely by your thoughts. The "What If" thinking can cause an overload of feelings and most are of negative nature.

Today is the day you are going to embark on the journey of facing your fears. You start out saying, "What if" I can't get out if I need to? The next thing that happens is a feeling of numbness in the legs, shaking, heart palpitations, and fear. You then try to bury those feelings or keep yourself busy so you don't have to feel them any longer.

This has to stop in order for you to completely be free of fears and phobias.

You must:
1. Recognize the thought
2. Determine if it is rational or irrational
3. Express what you are feeling

4. Express it out aloud
5. Express it in writing
6. Express by expression

Do not keep your feelings locked up inside. They are your feelings and you have a right to express them. Suppressing your feelings can create adverse health effects, mentally and physically.

This one day in particular stands out to me. When I was going through my time with fears and limitations, I could not hold it in anymore. I was angry, sad, and scared; I remember pounding my bed so hard that I thought it would be flattened. While I was punching the pillow, I was releasing the feelings and what a relief it was. No longer was I going to be a prisoner within my own feelings.

Expressing your feelings is easily done by keeping a journal. Every day take 15 minutes to write down your good and bad feelings.

One exercise I often do with my clients is to have them write letters to the people they are angry or upset with. The act of writing and expressing how one feels is the healing, the letter does not have to be given to the person, as it only needs to be released. If you have been holding in feelings with regard to someone else or holding a grudge, the healthy thing to do is write a letter. This will bring you clarity and alleviate the stored up stress and anxiety.

Express your feelings and never be afraid, you owe it to yourself to be clear and content.

DAY 26
Introduction to the Fearless You

D ay 26 is the establishment of the fearless you. What a magnificent transformation you have made. As we approach the end of this boot camp, I am sure you will be filled with a variety of emotions. One thing to be said is if you have been anxious throughout this boot camp, it is only normal. It will dissipate.

When you have fears and phobias it is assumed you have avoided certain places, situations, or objects. This is what has kept you in fear. In the midst of fear, came excuses that we talked about in an earlier segment. As you begin to take presence in the new fearless you, it is not uncommon to feel strange as though you are missing something. The grand thing is, you are not missing anything but what was holding you back from living.

You will feel different but don't let that intimidate you at all, this is all normal. Others may notice a change in you before you do. Embrace the changes that are being acknowledged.

At the same time as you are evolving into this positive and fearless person and celebrating the changes you have made, there is something you should be prepared for. It is unfortunate to say the very least, but oftentimes when there are positive changes in a person, the people around them are not happy. Happy may not be the right word, confused and intimidated may be better. The people you have relationships with whether it be family or friends, they are used to you being a certain way. When you make changes, they may try to bring you down or even ridicule you. This is sad but very true.

Amy had finally made the decisions to work on conquering her fears and being vulnerable to them. She decided to give up the excuses and be positive and move forward in life. She was elated that she had made the commitment and succeeded.

Her best friend for 10 years was not as thrilled as Amy was. She felt that Amy was not the same person and she felt threatened by her. It seemed every time Amy told her friend to think positive and to believe in herself, she would make comments that would be negative toward Amy.

Amy was upset over this and did not quite understand why her friend was not happy for her and she made her feel foolish at times. It occurred to Amy that her friend was a very negative person and she liked that Amy too be this way, therefore, making her friend feel better about herself.

For Amy to continue on with a positive outlook and to remain in a fear-free life, she had to sever ties with her friend. At first it was heartbreaking but after she really thought about it, she realized that her friend was actually helping her stay in fear.

Even family members can bring you down. It is imperative at this time to write down who you feel is negative and could bring you down.

_____

_____

_____

_____

_____

Do you feel comfortable standing up for yourself with these people and asking them to try being positive?

Who do you think will admire you for your efforts?

_____

_____

_____

Who do you think will not accept the new you as readily?

_____

_____

_____

Why would the names of the people you wrote down not accept the new you?

_____

_____

_____

You have reached the day where you have developed positive habits and changes in your life to live life fully and you are excited. It is natural to think that people all around you would rejoice as well. Most people will be pleased by your changes but there are others who may not know how to handle them. This is not your issue, it is theirs. Anyone who is not overjoyed for you should be reconsidered as a friend. It is as simple as that.

When you are entering the world of being fearless you will need a support system. This support system must be made up of positive, motivating, and encouraging people. If you do not find this, you need to seek out positive people.

It may sound to you that there are negative effects by positive changes and living without fear. There is nothing negative about it. You will become aware of how negative the people around you may have been and at one time, it made you feel better. Now that you are confident and motivated to live life in a more positive and empowering way, you may weed out the people who have been dragging you down and in essence contributing to you living in fear.

The realizations of these findings are going to be what separates you from falling backwards. There will always be the risk of setbacks and this is normal. If you can distance yourself from negative people, the chances of setbacks are much less.

There is another side to this. The friends and family members that may have had a hard time with your transformation will want to follow your lead. They will ask for your help to guide them to a more positive life. This is remarkable, but it may not be immediate; it could take time for people to see the benefits and to have them recognize their own fears and negativity.

Embrace these wants from others as it will make you grow more and raise your confidence even more.

Being a coach who works with people with anxiety disorders, fears, phobias, and low self-esteem, this is a known fear for them. I all too often hear, "If I get better and change, will anyone like me?" "Will I be the same person?" Think of these two questions and ask yourself if you have thought about them before.

Allow me to explain, you are the same person at the core but you are an improved person living the way you should be. We were not put on this earth to fear life, we were put here to live life and learn and enjoy. You are not a different person; you have made amazing strides and changes in this boot camp. You are yourself but much improved!

Freedom from Fear

D ay 27, I can hardly believe you are here already. What an amazing journey I hope you have had. You are now embarking on a life without fear. This is real, you have done it. You can go on from here without fear. You are free.

What does freedom from fear mean to you?

_____

_____

_____

_____

_____

Is the glass half empty or half full?

_____

What can you do now that you *would* not have done before this boot camp?

_____

_____

_____

_____

As you enter into your new world without fear, do not look back. Do not look back at what could have been if you hadn't wasted time in fear. None of that matters anymore. Fear is now in your past. Lost time is in your past. All that matters now is your present and your future. Your future is now full of opportunities and open doors.

Allison was an agoraphobic; she left her house only to collect the mail. She spent her days inside quivering at the mere thought of leaving her home. She was 28 years old.

Allison spent her days in desperation of finding a way out; she found my Web site and sent me an email. This was a changing time for Allison and me. As her coach, we worked together to define her fears and break them down into small pieces. This way they did not look so mammoth and untouchable to her. The process began.

Allison started out slow and the first place she went was the corner store. She had gone with her brother; the store was a mile away. She had not been in a car in 2 months; this was a gigantic stretch for her. We had visualized her leaving the house and it was the day she was taking action.

The ride to the store was much faster than she had thought, she was pleasantly surprised. Allison and her brother arrived at the store and she was hesitant to go inside, but she knew there would be a reward inside. She loved Snicker's bars and she wanted one, but in order to get one, she had to go in the store. Her brother refused to go inside for her.

She was left with two choices: Not receiving her reward (Snicker's bar) or going inside and getting much more than a Snicker's bar. She took a huge breath in and put her foot outside of the car and walked. She walked right in that store and grabbed her Snicker's bar. She went up to the counter and the woman working asked her how she was and Allison replied, "I am free and fabulous today." This was the first day of Allison's new life. Not to say that Allison was instantly cured from that point on, but this is when she believed she could do it.

Within 1 month, Allison had gotten a full-time job and was living life. She went through the same process as in this boot camp and she succeeded and so can you.

If you were Allison, would you have gone in the store?

_____

If you said yes, what made you go in the store?

_____

_____

If no, what stopped you from going in the store?

_____

_____

_____

When you let go of your fears and phobias, you have one thing.....freedom. Living in NH where the state motto is: "Live Free or Die" and it is printed on our license plates, I see this daily. When you stop and think about this motto, it really applies to all of us. If you live in fear, you are not really living, so essentially part of you dies. So let's concentrate on only living free.

Below please find a list of truths when we are free of fear.

1. The sky is the limit
2. You can come and go as you please
3. You can be whatever you want to be
4. You can live life instead of letting it pass you by
5. You can look forward to things
6. You can conquer the world
7. You will achieve all of your goals
8. You will be happy
9. You will be fulfilled
10. You will be busy
11. You can help others
12. You will be a better you

The list is endless. Have you made your choice?

_____

Take a moment and think of all your potential now that you are free from fears and phobias. Can you see them all?

Please list them below.

_____

_____

_____

_____

_____

_____

Don't just imagine your life free of fear, Live it! You can do it! Believe in yourself and the new you.

Discipline

iscipline is not only for children, it is for all ages. There are variations to discipline and we are going to talk about how to discipline you after becoming fearless.

Oftentimes instead of keeping the effort going when trying to confront fears or break bad habits it is easier to fall back to old ways. Don't do it! You are going to have to keep yourself in check at all times until the new habits and ways of thinking are embedded into you.

From the first day of this 30-day boot camp, we have gone through many stages and introductions to new habits. Once you finish this boot camp, those efforts cannot stop there. You must continue to follow the steps until they are second nature. It only takes a short 28 days to create a new habit as well as break one; this should not be a problem for you at all.

If you find yourself starting to think like you did before in a negative manner, you must stop yourself immediately. There is no longer a need for negative or fearful thoughts. Think of the visualization that you should have created right away if the negative shows its ugly head.

Even now that you are fearless, you will still have good and bad days. If you have bad days, do not dwell on them. Do not let old habits back in. Ask yourself these questions:

1. Why did I have a bad day?
2. What can I do to make it better tomorrow?
3. Was I thinking negative or positive?

This will keep you on the right path. Yes, I know it is work, but we are all a work in progress.

What if I fall backwards? What if I get anxious? These are questions that I know you will ask yourself at some time; the answer to any "What if" question, should be, "So what if!?" It changes the dynamic instantly, it is no longer negative.

Disciplining yourself is what is going to afford you a fearless life forever. By adopting the tools in this boot camp and following through with motivation and commitment, you will minimize the risk of any setbacks.

In 2005, I had achieved the biggest goal of my life: healing myself from anxiety. During my recovery process, my 30 year old cousin, Ryan, was diagnosed with colon cancer. You can only imagine the fears that surrounded me after learning this as he was younger than me. As time went on and he began his treatments, I had to tell myself over and over again, I only have anxiety, he has cancer. It had to be put into perspective.

His health was declining and the cancer had spread to his liver. My sister, mother, and I went to see him. As I sit here now, I remember my nervous belly and anticipation of how I was going to feel when I saw him. During the ride to his home, I kept rehearsing the same mantra, "I am going to be fine, this is not about me" over and over again. We were all nervous but I was particularly vulnerable because I was not yet at the end of my healing.

In this instance, I had two choices, I could forget about myself and my fears and go see my cousin, which could be the last time or I could hide in fear and regret it for the rest of my life. There was no way I was going to put myself first, this was about him.

Walking in the door and seeing him sit at the kitchen table all yellow and ill was shocking to say the least. It was hard at first to look at him, but we all adjusted. Sitting there was a 30 year old man who had just gotten out of the Navy and was facing the biggest fear one can have. He was so positive and grateful; he changed my life that day. His attitude was not one of fear it was one of living.

Ryan did not win his fight against cancer, but he sure taught us all a lot. He had choices too, he could give up or he could fight; he fought, but did not win. He died with dignity and strength no less.

This is where you need discipline, not to let your thoughts get in the way of what you have to do. He passed away about 4 months after I saw him at his house that day. The next challenge was going to his funeral.

This was a relatively minor challenge as compared to what might have been before because I stayed disciplined. I walked into that funeral parlor and I was sad but strong. What could have happened was after seeing him in such an ill-stricken state, I could have reverted back to my fears and erased all of what I had taught myself. This did not happen; it empowered me to fight on until I was free. This was done by discipline.

Every day new things come our way; some are great and some not so great. It is the times that are not great that you must be vigorous with your discipline. It would be no good to go through this book camp and be given tools and suggestions if you disregard them.

In your opinion, what is going to be the hardest part of disciplining yourself?

_____

_____

What can you do to make it easier for you?

_____

_____

Discipline involves structure, routine, and also praise. Always give yourself praise when you feel it due. Praising yourself is just as important as disciplining yourself. You can compare this somewhat to a diet.

You begin a diet and you have written down your menus for each week. You keep a log of the food and the amount of calories you ate each day. You dismiss yourself from having the chocolate cake because you are disciplining yourself. You have a goal in mind and you must be disciplined to reach it. Each week you step on the scale to see your progress or lack thereof. If you have lost weight, you praise yourself, if you gained weight, you need more discipline.

This is no different that disciplining yourself against old demons and bad habits coming back! You have grown so much in these last several days; I have no doubt in you!

Remember, discipline and praise!

Making Decisions

Making decisions can be stressful. Oftentimes, decision making is accompanied by doubts and fears. This Day 29 is to help you in making clear and long-lasting decisions.

Have you ever struggled with a decision you had to make?

_____

What surrounded the struggle?

_____

_____

_____

How did you ultimately come to making your decision?

_____

_____

_____

There are millions of different times we are presented with making decisions. Some are easy, some require consequences. If you have a decision to make that may affect your life, it should be thought out and looked at from all angles. Life decisions should not be made in haste. They should be well thought out.

If you make a quick decision and it ends up being the wrong decision, undoubtedly you will have to pay the price.

On this Day 29, decision making is imperative as you are going to have to make many more decisions now that you are free. One vital element in making decisions is once the decision is made, you must stand behind it. It was made by you and you must live with it, good or bad.

Some decisions are easy to make, like what to have for dinner or what movie to watch. While others can be complex and require research and thought processing.

Paul, who had a fear of being on the highway, was asked by his friend to go to the beach with a group. There was only one way to get to the beach and that was by the highway. Paul had to make the decision whether he was going to go and have fun with friends or stay home to avoid the highways.

Paul did not have much time to think about it as they were leaving in an hour from when he got the call. No matter what Paul's decision would be, he had to accept it as he was the one making the decision. It was unfortunate that Paul made the decision not to go on this occasion due to his fear. He felt horrible and foolish after and decided he would take the risk. He then tried to call his friend back but they had already left. He was upset with himself and he beat himself up all day.

Paul called me that night and told me about it and I proceeded to explain to him he made the decision not to go

and he has to let it go after that. Fretting ovᴇ.
could have done will not make the situation brighter. It ıs
over and done with. What Paul learned from this indeci-
sion was that he was at the helm and was responsible for
his own decision; therefore, he would really think about
it more before he lost another enjoyable opportunity.

As you get out into the fearless world you can easily be
influenced to make decisions that are not really yours.
Outsiders can try to sway you one way or another. At
times they may have great angles as to why you should
decide one way or another, but at other times the reasons
can only be selfish. You must be careful of this. Once
most decisions are made, they are final. You cannot go
back in time.

The same applies when making the decision to change;
you cannot turn back once you have made your decision.
You picked up this boot camp and now you have made
a decision that you want to eliminate your fears. If you
chose this book, this is the right time for you to take
charge. You have made a life-changing decision.

We have all made bad decisions throughout our lives, but
it is these decisions that help us learn and grow. If you
make a decision that you feel is wrong, accept it and
learn from it. It is all a learning process.

Follow these steps when making a life-changing decision:

1. Ask yourself what is the desired outcome?
2. How will this decision affect you in the long term?
3. Will the decision allow you to move forward?
4. Can you live with this decision?
5. Can you accept this decision?
6. Are you clear about your decision?

You will have decisions to make every day from what to
wear, what to eat, when to go to bed, and so forth; each

decision is your own and that is the key. Don't let other people make decisions for you; you are the captain of your life in small and large decisions.

Always be clear on your decisions and always accept them as yours, good or bad.

DAY 30 Congratulations to YOU!

You made it to the end! I am so proud of you. You owe yourself a big round of applause. On this last day, we are going to recap what we have been talking about along the way.

I am sure this process wasn't a bed of roses but it is commendable that you have stuck it out and moved forward. You identified your fears and phobias; on this Day 30, please write down how you feel today about what you wrote down on Day 1.

_____

_____

_____

_____

If the fear is still there, do you have a better understanding what you need to do to eliminate it?

_____

How is your thinking today, positive or negative?

_____

Have you been more aware of your thoughts and how to change the negatives to positives?

_____

If you are still struggling with changing your thoughts go back and re-read the sections on positive thinking. It is okay to have to repeat portions if need be, this is yours to keep. I encourage you to refer back often.

Have you set attainable goals?

_____

Are there still goals that you would like to reach?

_____

What are the goals that you want as of today?

_____

_____

_____

What would you rate your confidence level as on a scale of 1–10?

_____

Are you satisfied with your level?

_____

Have you learned to love yourself more?

_____

You must love yourself to be truly happy in life. If you are not there yet, go back and redo the exercises that will help you along.

Are you writing a to do list daily?

_____

Make sure when writing your to do list, you have positive statements on every other line. This is very motivating and grounding.

Have you listened to clues regarding your purpose?

_____

Always listen to your intuition, it is invaluable.

You can have all that you want in life if you believe in yourself. If you don't believe in yourself then how can someone else?

What was the most helpful tool for you in this boot camp and why?

_____

_____

Don't forget about affirmations, they carry more power than you can imagine. Listed below are some that you should use. Cut them out, make copies and hang them everywhere. Repetition is key, say them at least three times a day.

1. I know that nothing is impossible for me.
2. I am more than others may think of me.
3. I am proud of who I am.
4. I am confident.
5. I am a success.
6. I can beat any fear.
7. I am fearless.
8. I love myself.
9. I was born to achieve.
10. I possess only strength and power over fear.
11. My opportunities are endless now.
12. I am free.
13. I love life.

14. I am more than okay.
15. I can do it.
16. I only think positive thoughts.

Create your own affirmations as well and put your name at the beginning. Always read and say out loud when waking up, in the middle of the day, and before bed.

It is inconsistent to feel fear or negativity when you are saying positive affirmations, this is easy and influential.

Remember that you are your safety. Affirmations will instill this in you. No other person can make you safe, safety comes from within.

Facing fears is hard, but not as hard as living with them. You have come all of this way to become fearless, it is time for you to celebrate and look forward to challenges. You have the tools, the confidence, and the power to create the fearless life that you so deserve.

It is with my best wishes that you are fearless now. If you are not, do not give up, it takes time. Please do not be upset if there is lingering fear, you will conquer them all.

I am so grateful to have had this opportunity to share this boot camp with you. It is my wish that nobody lives in fear any longer.

Life is grand. Go out and live it. I will be with you every step of the way. Please feel free to email me at any point during your boot camp for support. You are not alone. I have been in fear, but I have conquered my fears; you can do the same.

I believe in you and I wish you all the best.

lifecoachkbaker@aol.com

About the Author

Kristen L. Baker

In my life I have experienced many things, some wonderful, some painful and more that have helped me to be who I am today. In the year 2002, I began to experience anxiety. The trigger was an overwhelming amount of stress. The anxiety symptoms could have been stopped, but I let my thinking change it from normal anxiety to debilitating anxiety.

Days, weeks and months went by when my life had become limited. For me it was so hard to understand the "Why" I had this because I had been a successful businesswoman for many years, a mother, a wife, and a happy person. Knowing the why really would not change anything, it was the How to stop it, that was everything.

Through my year with anxiety, fears, and phobias, I learned more about myself, my strengths, and my weaknesses. Each day, even as painful as some were, I had learned something. I taught myself tools to cope and to change my thinking and reactions to situations. I helped myself back to living life, but more than that, I helped myself live life fearlessly.

In 2005, my first book was published, *It's Okay To Have Anxiety...Really*. I chose the title because I wanted people to know, it really is okay to have anxiety, everyone has it, and the key is how we handle it. Writing the book was so empowering for me, the best outcome was people being affected by it in a positive way.

In 2005, I studied and got my master Life Coach Designation. This was a turning point in my life, I was now going to do what I always wanted to do and that was to help others. In 2006, I took more courses and became a Life Coach for My Private Coach, the leader in the coaching industry. In 2007, I earned my Master Spiritual Coaching Designation. This has been an amazing journey for me and I owe it all to going through the anxiety and fearful living.

Join me on this 30-day journey, so you too can have a fearless life!

The amazing journey starts here!

Are you ready?

Ok....Come along on this amazing journey

30day BootCamp:
Your Ultimate Life Makeover

A step-by-step program that will teach you all of the tips, tricks, and techniques you need to get back in the driver's seat of your life.

Paperback $19.95
eBook $11.95

The Successful Introvert

This book will enable you (the introvert) to understand, appreciate, and celebrate your unique strengths.

Paperback $19.95
eBook $11.95

KRISTEN L. BAKER
M.L.C., M.S.L.C.

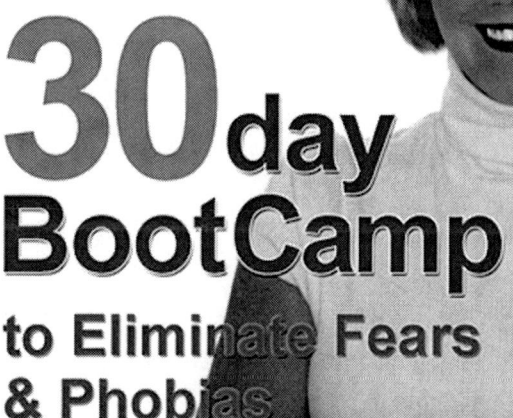

30day
BootCamp
to Eliminate Fears
& Phobias

If you enjoyed this book tell a friend!

To:

HappyAbout.info

Dear _____,

I just read a very cool book
called 30-DAY BOOT CAMP:
ELIMINATE FEARS AND PHOBIAS.
You should check it out.

Cheers

_____

(cut here)

Testimonials

"You are a wonderful writer and coach and I could not have beaten my anxiety without your loving support and knowledge. This book contains the wisdom and tools needed for anyone who is suffering from anxiety or fear to finally regain control of their life! You have a remarkable way of helping people and I am living proof that your methods and tools do work!! Thank you Kristen"
Jessica Hartman, NY

"Kristen is amazing. When I contacted her, I thought that I would never be able to live a full life. She, without hesitation said, you will and more in a couple of months. Someone once told me that we all have an angel, well Kristen has turned out to be mine. Not only am I living my life now without limitations, but I have found my purpose! One cannot put a price tag on that. Kristen brought me from encompassed with fear to be literally fearless in a very short time. Countless therapist and other coaches did nothing, but Kristen changed my life and my world. Thank you is not enough, I am forever grateful.
Carrie, United Kingdom

"It is funny that I am writing this about Kristen today because last week I had a major epiphany. I was driving to work and I thought to myself about my life exactly one year ago. I could not believe the person I was. I am in sense opposite to who I was one year ago. That is when I first talked to Kristen.

A year ago I was not driving on the freeways, I was living in constant fear, jumping at any noise, I did not like to socialize, I passed up many opportunities to go out with friends and meet new people, and being 26, this was important to me. I was working at an extremely stressful job, always crying or angry, and very jealous of other people. Today, I drive a total of 40 miles on the freeway everyday (IN THE FAST LANE!!), I have moved back to San Francisco, changed careers, and made some amazing friends. I am confident in myself, making new friends, meeting guys, and attending large events. I still have days with anxiety, but I have learned from Kristen to live in the moment and accept the feelings. I almost forgot to share what Kristen recently helped me overcome and this was major for me. I have had an extreme fear of flying for the past two years.

This last July I was invited on a fully paid one-week trip to Hawaii. I could not pass this up, but the 5 ½ hour flight haunted me every day. I had nightmares and at times thought I had to pull out of the trip. I emailed Kristen several times and she really gave me some great tips to help me through this. My doctor had prescribed Xanax for me to take for the flight. Finally the week had come and then the day had come and with Kristen helping me realize it is ok to feel anxious and that a lot of my feelings were merely excitement that I was confusing for anxiety I was able to enjoy the 5 ½ hour flight and NOT take the Xanax. I faced and overcame this fear without medication and with the help of Kristen."
Nicole, San Francisco

200 units y unt D

400 units / day

HighStreetN. com

Ab circle pro £129

Share weight

Lightning Source UK Ltd.
Milton Keynes UK
06 April 2010
152394UK00002B/46/P